Kuwait's Multibillion-Dollar Opportunities

A DEFINITIVE GUIDE FOR BUSINESS, EMPLOYMENT, AND INVESTMENT PARTICIPATION

Chetan and Sonal Shah
Global Marketing Intelligence, Portland, Oregon, U.S.A

A Division of Northwest Software, Inc.
P.O. Box 91396
Portland, Oregon 97291-0396

First Printing. Printed in the United States of America.

ISBN 1-880073-00-5

Library of Congress Catalog and Publication Data number: 91-72701

WARNING—DISCLAIMER

This guide is designed to provide information in regard to the subject matter covered. Such information has been obtained by the authors and publisher from sources believed to be reliable, at the time this edition was printed.

Every effort has been made to make this guide as complete and as accurate as possible. However, there may be mistakes—both typographical and in content. Furthermore, this guide contains information that is current as of the printing date. Therefore, this product should be used only as a general guide to business, employment, and investment participation in Kuwait. Other sources mentioned in the text of this guide should be consulted in order to complement the information provided herein, and to remain abreast of specific opportunities, and the market environment and changes.

This guide will help focus some of your efforts to seek and explore opportunities in Kuwait. However, it is not designed to be a get-rich-quick scheme. Like other companies and individuals who have successfully exploited opportunities in Kuwait, anyone else who decides to pursue such opportunities must expect to invest a lot of time and effort. Your success in Kuwait's marketplace hinges on the global competitiveness of your products or services and your business strategies.

It is not the purpose of this guide to reprint all the information that was otherwise available to the authors or publisher, but to complement, amplify, and supplement other material. For more information, see the many sources and references cited in the text and in the appendices.

The purpose of this guide is to educate and disseminate information that is relevant to the subject matter covered. The authors and publishers do not guarantee the accuracy, adequacy, or completeness of any information and are not responsible for any errors or omissions. The authors and publishers shall have neither liability nor responsibility to any person or entity with respect to any loss or damage caused, or alleged to be caused, directly or indirectly, from the use of the information contained in this guide.

WARNING—DISCLAIMER

About the Authors and Publisher

Northwest Software, Inc., the parent company of Global Marketing Intelligence, specializes in global product development, marketing, distribution, and international consulting.

The corporation founder's have a wealth of international experience in several areas including developing selected international markets, product distribution, planning and implementing strategic alliances across international boundaries and cultures, and management consulting on a variety of international business issues.

Prior to founding Northwest Software in 1988, the corporation founders worked for several years at Fortune 100 companies in a variety of industries. They have worked in, and have first-hand knowledge of, several international cultures.

In the product development and distribution process for international markets, Northwest Software, Inc. has developed a wealth of experience and gained a broad knowledge-base regarding a wide spectrum of international topics focused on developing countries.

Global Marketing Intelligence was formed as a division of Northwest Software, Inc. in order to assist other businesses and individuals develop and expand their market in rapidly developing international countries with significant potential in a broad range of industry sectors. *Kuwait's Multibillion-Dollar Opportunities* is the first in a series of such efforts.

Preface

Companies and individuals worldwide are now focusing on opportunities in the Middle East, especially Kuwait's multibillion-dollar postwar market. In March 1991, the U.S. Department of Commerce reported "Kuwait's reconstruction cost is between $60 billion and $100 billion, and the Kuwait Government has said U.S. companies and individuals will be favored in contracting for the 5-year rebuilding program. U.S. suppliers (businesses and individuals) of goods and services who meet international standards ... should find excellent market opportunities as a result of Kuwait's misfortune."

Kuwait's Multibillion-Dollar Opportunities is a definitive 112-page guide to seek and effectively compete in Kuwait's postwar business, employment, and investment opportunities. Targeted at U.S. business practitioners, job seekers, and investors, this guide provides focused information on identifying and competing in specific opportunities in an efficient and cost-effective manner, thereby saving valuable time and money.

This guide presents information on identifying and competing for three types of opportunities while rebuilding Kuwait: business, employment, and investment. Through its seven chapters and nine appendices, *Kuwait's Multibillion-Dollar Opportunities* provides valuable information.

Topics include: identifying and exploring specific products or services, employment, and investment opportunities; analysis of major market sectors and a framework to tap into those markets; cultural "do's and dont's"; taxation, visa, tariff and non-tariff regulations; U.S. and Kuwaiti sources of free or low-cost assistance to sell in Kuwait; comprehensive directory of selected U.S. and Kuwaiti companies participating in the rebuilding of Kuwait; and background information including Kuwait's social, economic, and government environment.

Chapter 1 describes potential business, employment, and investment opportunities in Kuwait's multibillion-dollar market. Chapter 2 identifies what these opportunities are specifically and points you in the right direction to pursue them.

Chapter 3 provides a comprehensive list of sources that can provide you low-cost or free assistance to successfully sell in Kuwait. Chapter 4 discusses the implications for U.S. businesses in Kuwait, and presents strategies for penetrating the market competitively. Chapter 5 describes Kuwait's foreign trade regulations and barriers.

Chapter 6 analyzes several market sectors, including oil and petrochemical, chemicals and catalysts, medical equipment and pharmaceuticals, telecommunications, and textiles and apparel. Chapter 7 provides general information about Kuwait, including its geography, government, economy, visa and travel requirements, and cultural do's and dont's.

The appendices contain a wealth of reference information. This includes such information as damages to the infrastructure; attractive industry segments; potential product and service classes with the most demand; U.S. Army Corps of Engineers subcontractors; directories such as key U.S. and Kuwaiti contacts, U.S. firms in Kuwait, and firms that have won contracts with the Kuwait Government, which may present subcontract or employment opportunites.

Acknowledgments

The list of authorities and sources consulted in the preparation of this book include departments of the U.S. and Kuwait Governments, libraries, industrial institutions, leading consultants, media members, newspaper and magazine articles and reports, press releases, and leading book distributors, book stores, publishers, and printers. We know that these people and organizations are proud to be a part of this effort to further the penetration of U.S. businesses and individuals in the Middle Eastern markets; thereby making a positive impact on our country's global competitiveness.

Global Marketing Intelligence wishes to sincerely thank all contributing organizations, individuals and sources, especially those identified below.

Key individuals that contributed to the development of this guide include Roy Armour, Sonal Shah, Kerry Koopman, Sameer Shah, Chetan Shah, and several Northwest Software, Inc. employees. The information was primarily researched and compiled by Sonal and Chetan Shah. Roy Armour focused his efforts on making this guide user-friendly. He led the effort to organize, edit, and format it. Additional contributions, including extensive reviews, were made continually by Kerry Koopman, Sameer Shah, and Chetan Shah. Valuable comments provided by members of the U.S. Department of Commerce and the Oregon Marketplace were incorporated.

Special thanks are also due to the U.S. Department of Commerce, Kuwaiti officials, and media members who helped increase the awareness and usefulness of this guide, thereby motivating U.S. businesses and individuals to participate in the opportunities present in Kuwait.

Further, the following works served as source material and contain additional information that may be helpful to you:

Jane Walker, ed. *Business Traveller's Handbook: A Guide to the Middle East*. NY, NY: Facts of Life, 1981.

Graham and Trottman. *Arab Business Yearbook*. Detroit, MI: Graham and Trottman, Ltd, 1986.

Roger E. Axtell, *Do's and Taboos of Hosting International Visitors*, Wiley, 1990.

"Employment Information." U.S. Department of Commerce, International Trade Administration, March 11, 1991, JBJ/3-11-91 Rev 2.

"Gulf Reconstruction — Commercial Information." U.S. Department of Commerce, International Trade Administration, March 18, 1991.

"International Trade Administration/US&FCS District Offices." U.S. Department of Commerce, March 1991, DEN-7-2/HANDOUT2.

"Kuwait Emergency and Recovery Program." Government of Kuwait, undated, KERPCOV.1.

Gulf Reconstruction Center. *Kuwait Restored Initiative 1991 Marketing Plan.* Washington, DC: U.S. Department of Commerce, February 28, 1991.

"Kuwait — Warning." U.S. Department of State, Bureau of Consular Affairs, March 13, 1991, Travel Advisory 91-067.

"Middle East, Africa, South Asia — Caution." U.S. Department of State, Bureau of Consular Affairs, March 10, 1991, Travel Advisory 91-061.

"OPIC Programs for U.S. Companies Participating in the Reconstruction of Kuwait." Overseas Private Investment Corporation, undated.

"Restoration of the Government of Kuwait Municipal Facilities." U.S. Army Corps of Engineers, February 19, 1991, No. 91-05.

"U.S. Army Corps of Engineers Contract Awards." U.S. Department of Commerce, International Trade Administration, March 12, 1991, Job312Fm 3-12-91.

Notes

Table of Contents

■ APPENDICES

Notes

1 MULTIBILLION-DOLLAR OPPORTUNITIES

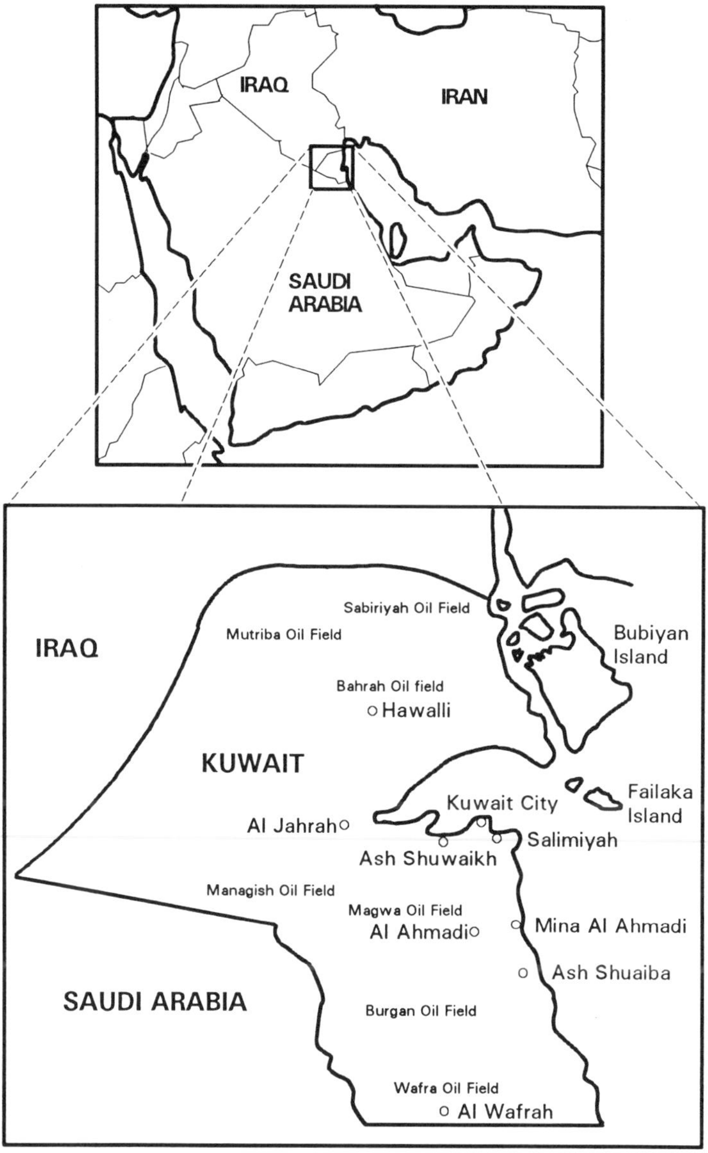

■ OVERVIEW

The outbreak of the Persian Gulf War focused the world's attention on the Middle East. The Iraqi and coalition force bombing completely destroyed the Kuwaiti infrastructure and caused better than $20 billion in damages. In March 1991, the U.S. and Kuwait Governments have estimated that reconstruction and restoration will cost between $60 and $100 billion.

During the course of the war, the Iraqis set hundreds of Kuwaiti oil wells ablaze and destroyed or vandalized many of its major buildings, businesses, and shops. Further, the Iraqis looted Kuwait's gold stocks and art treasures worth over $2 billion.

Appendix A identifies the major damage categories that need restoration. The damage created during the war was unfortunate. However, it presents substantial and renewed business, employment, and investment opportunities—especially for U.S. firms and individuals since the U.S. played a leading role in liberating Kuwait.

■ BUSINESS, EMPLOYMENT, AND INVESTMENT OPPORTUNITIES

Companies and individuals worldwide are now concentrating on opportunities in the Middle East, especially Kuwait's multibillion-dollar market. Given that the U.S. played a leading role in Kuwait's liberation, it is expected that (all other things being equal), U.S. firms and citizens will be favored for reconstruction contracts and other opportunities.

The reconstruction of Kuwait opens up exciting business, employment (for skilled and unskilled labor), and investment opportunities for U.S. firms and individuals in a diverse range of industries—see Appendix B for major industry segments with maximum potential. Product and service categories that are expected to provide significant sales opportunities are listed in Appendix C.

The window of opportunity for these industries, products, and services is expected to last at least until 1995.

Three types of opportunities result from the rebuilding, restocking, and restoring of Kuwait. These opportunities are:

- Business—sale of products and services.
- Employment—skilled and unskilled labor.
- Investment—joint ventures, licensing, etc.

Contracts worth $900 million already awarded!

Immediately following the war, the Kuwaiti government awarded the U.S. Army Corps of Engineers a $45 million contract, since increased to $100 million, to assess the damage and lead its initial rebuilding efforts.

As of May 1991, several other contracts worth over $900 million have already been awarded—over 70 percent to U.S. firms. This represents a small fraction of the total estimated market. Therefore, the window of opportunity in this multi-billion-dollar market is wide open. Several U.S. suppliers of goods and services are aggressively seeking market opportunities in Kuwait.

■ REBUILDING KUWAIT—THE PLAN

Given the magnitude of destruction and looting, the task of rebuilding Kuwait is expected to pose substantial challenges and opportunities through 1995. While Kuwait's rebuilding efforts are expected to last several years, the initial rebuilding plan has been divided into two 90-day phases.

- The first 90-day phase focused on restoring basic services, providing emergency relief, and assessing the damage.
- During the second phase, the emphasis shifted to restoring basic health care, sanitation, communications and utilities (food, water, and so on).

Phase I

■ During the first 90 days after the war, the focus was on restoring basic services, emergency relief and damage assessment. Immediately following the war, the Kuwaiti government contracted with the U.S. Army Corps of Engineers to estimate the damage, clean-up facilities, clear rubble, and repair roads, bridges, seaports, and airports.

Additionally, the emphasis during this phase was placed on providing the people with food, water, and medicine; restoring communications; and extinguishing oil well and facility fires.

As stated earlier, hundreds of contracts, worth over $900 million, were awarded during Phase I.

Phase II

■ The second 90-day phase will include detailed damage assessment and reconstruction planning work. Extensive rebuilding, which is expected to last up to ten years, will begin during this phase.

Phase II will provide substantial opportunities to businesses and individuals who can help with the basic reconstruction and restoration needs of Kuwait's buildings, factories, warehouses, businesses, oil installations, and so forth.

Representative Phase I and Phase II projects

■ Examples of major projects that are expected to be underway at the end of Phase II include:

- Extinguishing hundreds of oil well and facility fires—a task that will require extensive labor and could last up to two years. Also, damaged control systems and wellhead valves will need repair or replacement.

- Reconstruction of government and commercial buildings, factories, warehouses, transportation facilities, and other structures.
- Rebuilding of telecommunications and computer-based information systems, and support facilities.
- Supply of basic necessities and services.
- Business support services.

Notes

2 TAPPING INTO THIS MULTI-BILLION-DOLLAR MARKET

Need help in identifying and pursuing specific opportunities within Kuwait's multibillion-dollar market? This section focuses on providing answers to the following two questions:

- What are the opportunities?
- How do you get started?

The information in this section, complemented with your marketing programs and quality products/services, will position you ahead of your competition in the Kuwaiti market.

Three types of opportunities are available within the Kuwaiti market:

- Business—sale of products and services.
- Employment—skilled and unskilled labor.
- Investment—joint ventures, licensing, etc.

TYPES OF BUSINESS OPPORTUNITIES

The scale of the reconstruction efforts to rebuild Kuwait has created the need for a diverse range of products and services. The target industry segments and products or services that hold maximum potential for providers of goods and services are provided in Appendices B and C, respectively.

Business opportunities to sell products and services into one or more target industries in Kuwait may be explored either as prime contractors or as subcontractors.

Thousands of businesses within the industry segments listed in Appendix B are competing for a piece of the multibillion-dollar market.

Millions of dollars in contracts have been awarded

While several large firms and agencies have already won multimillion-dollar contracts, smaller and medium-sized firms can also tap into the market by either subcontracting with prime contractors, or by contacting the Kuwaitis directly. Large U.S. firms and Government agencies that have already won Kuwaiti rebuilding contracts include:

- U.S. Army Corps of Engineers
- Bechtel Group, Inc.
- International Business Machines (IBM)
- Raytheon, Inc.
- Waste Management, Inc.

Appendix I contains a comprehensive list of small, medium, and large firms that have won contracts with the Kuwait Government.

Corps subcontract awards

The initial contracts made by the U.S. Army Corps of Engineers on behalf of the Kuwaiti reconstruction project have been subcontracted to several small, medium-sized and large firms (see Appendix D).

Since the Corps is expected to continue soliciting proposals for additional reconstruction work in Kuwait, it is recommended that firms and individuals seeking opportunities in Kuwait get on the Corps' mailing list (described later under "Increase awareness for your products or services").

Exploring business opportunities

■ The following paragraphs provide step-by-step information that you can use to explore the opportunities available in Kuwait.

This information, complemented with your competitive offerings and business strategies, should help you compete effectively with the thousands of businesses and individuals who are already attempting to explore Kuwaiti or other Middle East opportunities. This information is organized as follows:

- ☐ Increase awareness for your products, services, or skills.

- ☐ Obtain information on the major projects and market opportunities.
- ☐ Obtain information specific to your industry.
- ☐ Hire a registered local agent or representative.
- ☐ Develop an export plan.

Additional information on exploring opportunities in selected market sectors is provided in Chapter 6, "Analysis of Major Market Sectors".

Increase awareness for your products, services, or skills

In addition to your on-going marketing tactics to increase awareness and create a preference for your products/services, you should send information to the agencies listed below. These agencies will include your information in a database, which will be made available to the Kuwaiti government.

As projects are planned and implemented, the Kuwaitis are expected to contact qualified U.S. firms or individuals listed in the database. Contact information (including names, addresses and phone numbers) is provided in Appendix E—a convenient reference for key contacts.

- ☐ Commerce Department, Gulf Reconstruction Center. (See Appendix E under "U.S. Contacts".)

- ☐ Commerce Department, Office of the DAS for Basic Industries. (See Appendix E under "U.S. Contacts".)

- ☐ U.S. Army Corps of Engineers. If you are an Architecture, Engineering, Construction, or Supply firm, or a professional, you should contact the appropriate contact identified in Appendix E under "U.S. Contacts".

- ☐ Kuwait Emergency and Reconstruction Program (KERP). You should contact KERP for civil sector reconstruction projects. (See Appendix E under "Kuwaiti Contacts".)

- ☐ Kuwait Petroleum International. Use this contact for oil sector reconstruction projects. (See Appendix E under "Kuwaiti Contacts".)

In addition, you should pursue potential subcontracting opportunities by offering your products or services through selected prime contractors (see Appendices G and I).

Another way to effectively increase your awareness is to participate in selected trade shows and events. In this way, you can meet potential customers as well as assess your competitors.

The Commerce Department creates U.S. presence at international trade fairs to make it easier for U.S. firms to exhibit and gain recognition internationally. For assistance in participating in trade show events, contact the Commerce Department's Regional Export Development Office nearest to you (see Appendix E, under "U.S. Contacts").

Obtain information on major projects and market opportunities

In addition to regularly monitoring trade and government publications, you should contact the following agencies periodically to remain abreast of current or planned projects and market opportunities.

- ☐ State Department, American Embassy Kuwait. Send your correspondence to the Commercial Specialist or to the Commercial Attache. (See Appendix E under "U.S. Contacts".)

- ☐ Commerce Department—contact the Desk Officer for Kuwait. (See Appendix E under "U.S. Contacts".)

- ☐ Trade associations. Contact the U.S.-Arab Chamber of Commerce in Washington, D.C. (See Appendix E, "Other Organizations" under "U.S. Contacts".)

Obtain information specific to your industry

Information specific to most industries may be obtained from the Commerce Department's, International Trade Administration, United States and Foreign Commercial Services (USFCS) office.

To become more knowledgeable about market opportunities and potential for your specific industry, you should contact the appropriate USFCS office in Washington D.C. (see Appendix F for a list of industries and USFCS phone numbers). Appendix F also lists the USFCS district offices that can provide export assistance for your products or services.

Hire a registered local agent or representative

If you plan to sell directly to Kuwait, you must consider hiring a registered local agent or representative.

The Commerce Department's Agent Distributor Service (administered through the USFCS), can provide assistance in locating and selecting an agent, distributor, or representative in Kuwait. An in-country agent or representative is required because it is:

- Usually required under Kuwaiti law.

- An excellent and inexpensive mechanism to identify and service sales opportunities efficiently. Further, it helps minimize risks associated with cultural differences.
- Essential for timely notification of major projects and tenders, and to maintain contact with ministry officials and decision makers.

Develop an export plan

After understanding the market potential, you must develop a structured plan to export your services or products to Kuwait, either directly or through a prime contractor.

While the development of a comprehensive plan is beyond the scope of this publication, the major elements of the plan must include:

- Selection and analysis of your target market, including potential, barriers to entry, competition, and regulations. As described earlier, several agencies (see Appendices E and F), can facilitate this task by providing you with the relevant data.
- Your export goals and strategies to achieve them.
- Customization of products or services for the Kuwaiti market if necessary.

- Development and implementation of a marketing program including public relations, direct mail, trade show participation, and targeted advertisements in trade publications.
- Budgets for marketing, travel, etc.
- Visits to meet with your Kuwaiti customers and agents or distributors, as necessary.

■ TYPES OF EMPLOYMENT OPPORTUNITIES

In addition to the business opportunities for selling U.S. products and services, substantial opportunities for job seekers and self-employed individuals are expected to become available.

You will find maximum opportunity in the industry segments listed in Appendix B. Such opportunities exist due to two major reasons:

- Before the war, 70 percent of the Kuwaiti registered labor force (skilled and non-skilled) consisted of non-resident aliens who fled to their native countries seeking shelter during the war. Such an exodus has created a large void in Kuwait's supply for skilled and unskilled labor.
- Increased need for employees because of the aggressive reconstruction efforts in several industries that require skilled and unskilled labor.

Exploring employment opportunities

■ Thousands of job applications have been received by several government agencies, prime contractors, and Kuwaiti businesses.

Those who are seeking to participate in Kuwait's reconstruction projects as individuals should maximize their exposure with the Kuwaiti government, prime contractors, and government agencies. These individuals should send their job applications for inclusion in a database that will be made available to Kuwaiti businesses and government agencies.

Individuals seeking employment and contract opportunities should write to the organizations described below in order to increase their exposure.

☐ **Kuwait Emergency Recovery Program (KERP)** Human Resource Database. The KERP office is maintaining a database of individuals seeking participation in Kuwait's recovery program. (See Appendix E under "Kuwaiti Contacts".)

☐ **Labor Department**. To manage the high volume of calls from individuals seeking employment in the Gulf region, the Labor Department has set up a toll-free line (800)927-5690. The Labor Department is also maintaining a database of individuals interested in participating in Kuwait's recovery program. This database will be made available to the Kuwait Government on a regular basis.

- ☐ **Interstate job bank**. The Labor Department encourages U.S. firms participating in Kuwait's reconstruction efforts to hire U.S. workers to the maximum extent possible and to list their job openings with the public employment service national interstate job bank. Therefore, individuals interested in Kuwait employment openings should contact their nearest public employment service (listed under the state government listings in the phone book) in order to take advantage of any relevant positions listed by employers.

- ☐ **U.S. firms doing business in Kuwait**. (See Appendices G and I.) Contact selected firms who are already doing business in Kuwait for business, subcontract, or employment opportunities.

- ☐ **Market your skills extensively**. In addition to submitting your applications to the above agencies, you must actively market your skills and services to prime and subcontractors (see Appendices G and I) who have won (or are about to win) Kuwaiti contracts.

■ TYPES OF INVESTMENT OPPORTUNITIES

Joint ventures and licensing arrangements with Kuwaiti firms are an effective means to enhance Kuwait's global competitiveness since goods and services produced locally can substitute for imports.

- **Joint ventures**—equity ownership in most joint ventures is usually limited to 49 percent by non-Kuwaiti firms and individuals. Advantages that can accrue to such ventures are management control, limited liability for the partners, and possible shelter from Kuwaiti corporate taxes.
- **Licensing arrangements**—usually include a lump-sum fee for the transfer of technology and a royalty payment for the repeated use of technology. The lump-sum and royalty fees are both negotiated and are usually limited by governmental regulations.

The Kuwait Government encourages such strategic alliances in order to import state-of-the-art technology, while adding maximum value within the country. The Kuwait Government's plan to develop a major petrochemical industry in Kuwait poses potential opportunities for profitable alliances between U.S. and Kuwaiti businesses.

Other possibilities for investment are the local futures markets for foreign exchange and gold bullion. Participation in

Kuwait's real-estate and equity markets is limited to Kuwaiti nationals only.

Exploring investment opportunities

■ Most opportunities for strategic alliances are usually negotiated by high level management of the two firms. To pursue your interest in strategic alliances and investment opportunities contact:

- ☐ Overseas Private Investment Corporation in Washington, D.C. (See Appendix E, "Other Organizations" under "U.S. Contacts".)
- ☐ Top-level management of Kuwaiti firms within your industry.
- ☐ Your investment broker for information on potentially attractive financial investments in Kuwait.

■ WHERE TO LOOK FOR OPPORTUNITIES

Individuals and businesses interested in pursuing opportunities in Kuwait should regularly scan the following sources of additional information. These sources will provide further insight into specific opportunities (business, employment or investment). Most publications are available in major libraries.

Additional sources of opportunities described in this section include trade events and the Economic Bulletin Board (EBB).

U.S. firms doing business in Kuwait or the Middle East

U.S. firms already in the area have experience working with the Kuwaitis and as such, have a greater potential for success in winning contracts. You may contact these firms for potential employment or subcontract opportunities (see Appendices G and I).

U.S. publications

- *Commerce Business Daily*
- *Engineering News Record*
- *Journal of Commerce*
- *New York Times*
- *Wall Street Journal*
- Trade publications and journals specific to your industry.

Foreign publications

- *Middle East Business Intelligence*—contains information about upcoming projects and tenders in the Middle East.
- *Middle East Economic Digest*–provides extensive information on contracts finalized by foreign firms in Middle Eastern countries.

Other publications

While a selected list of U.S. companies operating in Kuwait is provided in Appendices G and I, several publications and directories provide a more comprehensive list of U.S. firms operating abroad. Some such publications and directories include:

- Uniworld Business Publications, 50 E. 42nd Street, Suite 509, NY, NY 10017-5480, Phone: (212)697-4999.
- Standard and Poors business directories.

Trade events

The Commerce Department sponsors trade events and catalog shows in the Persian Gulf region. For more information and assistance, contact the Commerce Department's Regional Export Development Center (see Appendix E, under "U.S. Contacts").

Economic bulletin board

The EBB can be accessed 24 hours each day for information on a variety of topics, including daily trade opportunities. For more information on the EBB, contact your local Commerce Department office, or call the EBB staff at (202)377-1986.

■ FINANCE AND INSURANCE ASSISTANCE

The Overseas Private Investment Company (OPIC) has instituted a special program to provide financial assistance for small businesses and contractors intending to do business in Kuwait and other Persian Gulf countries.

The OPIC Financial Assistance Program assists small businesses with obtaining standby letters of credit and other such instruments necessary in conducting international business.

The OPIC Insurance Program helps minimize the risks associated with doing business in the Gulf region. The insurance offered under this program can protect a wide range of U.S. service providers.

Contact OPIC for additional information. (See Appendix E, "Other Organizations" under "U.S. Contacts".)

Notes

3 SOURCES FOR HELP AND ASSISTANCE

Several U.S. and Kuwaiti agencies are available to help U.S. firms explore business opportunities in the Persian Gulf. This chapter provides a comprehensive list of sources that can help businesses and individuals participate in rebuilding Kuwait.

Contact information (including names, addresses and phone numbers) for these sources mentioned are provided in Appendix E—a convenient reference for key contacts. Potential sources of cost-effective assistance include:

- U.S. Government agencies
- Kuwait Government agencies
- Overseas Private Investment Corporation
- Trade associations.

■ U.S. GOVERNMENT AGENCIES

The U.S. Government has made a strong commitment to improve America's trade performance by expanding exports, which is now a national priority.

Gulf Reconstruction Center

Given the tremendous export potential, the Commerce Department has established the Gulf Reconstruction Center to provide focused assistance to tap into Middle East opportunities. The Gulf Reconstruction Center is the most important organization and the best place to start pursuing opportunities in Kuwait or in other Middle East countries.

The Gulf Reconstruction Center can provide you with up-to-date information on how to participate in Kuwait's rebuilding efforts. The Center is currently developing a database of businesses and individuals interested in selling products or services in Kuwait.

The Center accepts information that describes your products or services and will pass it along to the Kuwait Government and other interested Kuwaiti companies.

International Trade Administration

The International Trade Administration (ITA), a U.S. Department of Commerce office, is the primary U.S. agency responsible for assisting U.S. businesses to export products and services.The ITA's export promotion services (described in detail in Appendix H) include:

- Export counselling
- Agent/Distributor service
- Commercial news USA

- Foreign buyer program
- Gold key service
- Trade opportunities program
- World traders data report
- Overseas catalog and video-catalog shows
- Overseas trade missions
- Overseas trade fairs
- Matchmaker events.

ITA units of interest. There are three ITA units of interest. These are identified below and described in the following paragraphs:

- U.S. and Foreign Commercial Services
- Trade Development Unit
- International Economic Policy Unit.

U.S. and Foreign Commercial Services Unit

The U.S. and Foreign Commercial Services (USFCS) has 47 district and 21 branch offices in the U.S (see Appendix F for contact information). These offices can provide assistance and information about market opportunities in the Persian Gulf.

To promote U.S. products and services, the USFCS can forward corporate information to USFCS offices located in Persian Gulf countries. This information is then made available to Kuwaiti firms and government agencies.

Since several Middle East firms seeking U.S. products and services contact the local USFCS offices, these offices can be an important source of leads for business opportunities. The USFCS offices can also provide assistance in the following areas:

- Conducting customized market research.
- Providing information on specific business opportunities and trade barriers (if any).
- Qualifying sales agents and distributors.
- Scheduling appointments with commercial and government prospects.
- Obtaining export license and financing.
- Appointing an overseas representative.
- Obtaining credit rating for overseas prospects and customers.
- Complying with customs regulations.

Trade Development Unit

The Trade Development Unit promotes the global trading interests of selected

U.S. industry sectors and offers information on markets and trade practices including:

- Trade, finance, and investment opportunities.
- Strategies to take advantage of Middle East opportunities.
- Bidding on a large project.

For more information, contact the ITA Regional Export Development Officer in Washington, D.C. (See Appendix E under "U.S. Contacts".)

International Economic Policy Unit

The International Economic Policy Unit is a good source for information concerning the trade potential in specific countries.

This unit has a desk officer (or specialist) assigned to each country in the world. These officers can provide you information or assistance in the following areas:

- Foreign government regulations.
- Import and export tariffs and license requirements.
- Business practices.
- Economical and political developments.
- Market size and growth.

– Trade and investment agreement negotiations.

For more information, contact the International Economic Policy Unit's Kuwait Desk Officer. (See Appendix E under "U.S. Contacts".)

■ KUWAIT GOVERNMENT AGENCIES

Several Kuwaiti agencies can provide information on several aspects of doing business in Kuwait, business opportunities, and processes.

These agencies include the various ministries and the agency for Kuwait Emergency and Reconstruction Program (see Appendix E under "Kuwaiti Contacts").

■ OVERSEAS PRIVATE INVESTMENT CORPORATION

Contact the Overseas Private Investment Corporation (OPIC) office (see Appendix E, "Other Organizations" under "U.S. Contacts"), for information regarding financial and insurance requirements of U.S. firms seeking to do business in the Persian Gulf. OPIC is an independent and financially self-supporting U.S.-owned corporation.

■ TRADE ASSOCIATIONS

The U.S.-Arab Chamber of Commerce (see Appendix E, "Other Organizations" under "U.S. Contacts"), is a good potential source of information for business and trade related matters in the Persian Gulf.

4 IMPLICATIONS FOR U.S. BUSINESSES AND INDIVIDUALS

Since the U.S. played a leading role in the liberation of Kuwait, U.S. firms and individuals have good prospects for winning Kuwaiti contracts, thereby increasing their profitability. Given the prominent role played by the U.S. in the allied coalition, it is expected that U.S. exports to Kuwait in the 1990s will outperform most other countries.

Prior to the Iraqi invasion of Kuwait, U.S. exports to Kuwait showed dramatic improvement—increasing 24 percent from $690 million in 1988 to $855 million in 1989 (see table on U.S. Trade with Near East and North African Arab Countries, 1988-1990). The total U.S. exports to Kuwait in 1989 was close to Japan's exports, a leading export country to Kuwait.

This chapter describes the implications for U.S. business within these subjects:

- Kuwait: A golden opportunity for U.S. firms and individuals.
- Opportunities in other Middle East countries.
- Penetrating the Kuwaiti market competitively.

- Arab boycott complications.

■ KUWAIT: A GOLDEN OPPORTUNITY FOR U.S. FIRMS AND INDIVIDUALS

Primary reasons that make the Kuwaiti market a golden opportunity for U.S. firms and individuals include:

- The multibillion-dollar market potential.
- Potential for improved sales and profitability.
- High Kuwaiti preference for U.S. products and services.
- The relative decline in the value of the U.S. dollar vis-a-vis other major currencies encourages Kuwaiti traders to look to the U.S. as an alternative to traditional European and Japanese suppliers.
- Limited threat from other foreign competitors.
- Market for products and services that are mature in the U.S.
- Favorable political and economical conditions.
- Liberal export licensing procedures.
- Limited trade barriers.
- Potential for a long-term market. The rebuilding efforts may last as long as five or ten years.

■ OPPORTUNITIES IN OTHER MIDDLE EASTERN COUNTRIES

As shown in the Table below, substantial potential exists for U.S. products and services in several other Middle-Eastern countries. (The information presented in the following table was produced by the U.S. Department of Commerce and compiled by the Bureau of the Census Office of the Near East on February 20, 1991). The Table provides a historical (1988-1990) review of U.S. trade performance with the Arab countries in the Near East and North Africa. The data in the Table includes special category commodities and re-exports.

U.S. Trade with Near East and North African Arab Countries 1988-1990 (Million Dollars)

	U.S. Exports			U.S. General Imports		
	1988	**1989**	**1990**	**1988**	**1989**	**1990**
Total Area	14,541.3	15,064.8	15,017.0	14,845.3	17,444.9	21,862.4
% of U.S. Total	4.5	4.1	3.8	3.4	3.7	4.4
Arab Countries:						
Near East	7,541.6	8,255.3	7,778.0	9,404.9	11,894.0	15,360.0
Bahrain	280.6	488.7	718.4	110.0	79.8	80.7
Iraq	1,156.1	1,173.5	731.8	1,605.4	2,408.3	3,014.5
Jordan	372.8	380.7	309.1	13.2	8.6	11.5
Kuwait	690.3	855.0	400.7	506.8	975.0	569.9
Lebanon	123.4	93.4	98.1	42.1	30.6	24.3
Oman	129.6	169.6	162.8	82.2	117.0	291.9
Qatar	98.7	100.7	114.7	0.6	50.4	52.8
Saudi Arabia	3,799.2	3,576.0	4,034.8	6,236.9	7,181.3	9,974.3
Syria	88.5	91.5	98.2	42.1	98.2	52.1
UAE	710.5	1,239.6	998.2	616.2	685.0	888.5
Yemen	85.5	78.7	111.2	129.8	258.9	399.5
North Africa	3,685.1	3,926.5	3,872.0	2,363.2	2,217.2	3,182.8
Algeria	732.6	758.5	947.7	1,972.2	1,836.4	2,645.3
Morocco	428.0	398.0	497.0	102.1	98.3	109.1
Libya	—	—	—	—	—	—
Tunisia	184.8	160.0	178.5	46.0	56.0	32.0
Egypt	2,339.7	2,610.0	2,248.8	242.9	226.5	396.4
Non-Arab Countries:						
Near East	3,320.6	2,890.7	3,367.0	3,076.3	3,333.7	3,319.6
Iran	73.1	60.0	166.5	8.3	8.6	7.0
Israel	3,247.5	2,830.7	3,200.3	3,068.0	3,325.1	3,312.6

■ PENETRATING THE KUWAITI MARKET

While it is expected that U.S. firms will be preferred over firms from other coalition countries, U.S. firms should recognize that the Kuwaiti market is highly competitive and is extremely price sensitive.

This paragraph describes what U.S. firms and individuals must consider in order to assess and outperform the competition, especially firms from other coalition countries. Key competitive considerations must include:

- Prior experience in the Gulf region.
- Presence of sales channels such as a strong relationship with an agent, distributor, or representative in the Gulf region.
- Quality products and services that meet international standards, especially Kuwaiti standards and specifications.

To penetrate the Kuwaiti market competitively, U.S. firms and individuals must implement strategies that address any weakness in the above areas. Specific recommendations that U.S. firms and individuals might consider include:

- Appoint a registered local agent or representative—normally required under Kuwaiti law. Local representation is usually essential for timely notification of major projects and tenders, and to maintain contact with ministry officials and decision makers. Use of the U.S. and Foreign Commercial Service's (USFCS) Agent Distributor Services is a good and inexpensive tool to establish initial contact with potential agents or distributors (see Appendix F for USFCS contact information).
- Make regular trips to Kuwait in order to understand market conditions and to build (or maintain) a relationship with intermediaries and potential customers. The importance of direct contacts in international business (including Kuwait) cannot be overemphasized. Prior to traveling to Kuwait, you should contact the Commerce Department to remain informed of any travel advisories and to obtain assistance in making your business trip successful.

See Chapter 2, "Tapping into this Multibillion-Dollar Market", for a more comprehensive list of possible actions you can take to penetrate the Kuwaiti marketplace.

■ ARAB BOYCOTT COMPLICATIONS

Before the Iraqi invasion, Kuwait's adherence to the Arab League boycott of Israel had prevented some U.S. firms from doing business in Kuwait.

The extent of the post-war enforcement of the Arab League boycott was unknown at the time this guide was published. The U.S. Department of Commerce believes that enforcement of the boycott will be abandoned by at least those Arab countries that were members of the allied coalition.

U.S. firms may encounter boycott procedures in certificates of origin, letters of credit, shipping documents, certain tender and contract provisions, and in requests to furnish information about the firm's business relationships.

For more information about boycott regulations or problems, contact the Office of Anti-boycott Compliance at (202)377-2381 or the Treasury Department's Office of the General Counsel at (202)566-5569 (see Appendix E under "U.S. Contacts").

Notes

5

FOREIGN TRADE REGULATIONS AND BARRIERS

The challenges of identifying, exploring, and competing for opportunities across international boundaries is complicated by several factors including global competition, regulatory forces, tariff and non-tariff trade barriers, and cultural differences.

Since Kuwait's economy depends on imported goods and services, its trade laws are liberal with minimal restrictions. However, import licenses are required for most private sector goods.

Further, exporters must be aware of tariff and non-tariff barriers imposed by the Kuwait Government to protect the local industry and economy.

In general, the Kuwaiti market is attractive to overseas businesses and individuals because it is open to global competition. Further, it has minimal restrictions on currency exchange and on the transfer of profits and dividends.

This chapter describes information on Kuwait's foreign trade regulations including:

- Tariff barriers

- Non-tariff barriers
- Taxation
- Treaties and bilateral agreements
- Foreign exchange control.

■ TARIFF BARRIERS

Most goods are subject to import levies assessed ad valorem on the CIF value. Such tariff barriers, designed to protect the local economy, range from four percent to a maximum of 30 percent.

Goods exempt from customs tariffs include nearly all foodstuffs, books and periodicals, movie films, gold and silver bullion, most live animals, and animal feeds.

Contact the Commerce Department (see Appendix E under "U.S. Contacts") for information on import tariffs for your specific products or services.

■ NON-TARIFF BARRIERS

The Kuwait Government imposes a number of non-tariff barriers in order to:

- Implement the Arab League boycott regulations (discussed in greater detail in Chapter 4, "Implications for U.S. Businesses and Individuals").
- Conform with standards and specifications of the Gulf Cooperation Council (GCC).
- Combat the importation of counterfeit products.

– Protect the local economy and consumers.

Primary non-tariff barriers include:

- ☐ Certificate of Origin
- ☐ Country of origin markings
- ☐ Arabic language requirement
- ☐ Electrical standards
- ☐ Other barriers

Certificate of Origin

A Certificate of Origin identifies the origin of manufacture of goods and services. When goods shipped from the U.S. are manufactured (totally or in part) elsewhere, then each country of manufacture must be identified in the certificate.

Certification may be obtained from one of the following organizations in order of priority:

– U.S.-Arab Chamber of Commerce.

– An embassy or consulate of any Arab country (except Egypt).

– Any U.S. Chamber of Commerce within the state of origin.

In all cases, the documents (letters of credit, invoices, etc.) should be certified by the Kuwait Embassy (Washington, D.C.) or the Kuwait Consulate (New York City).

Country of origin markings

Goods cannot be exhibited or sold in Kuwait unless the country of origin is clearly marked on the outside of the product. A sticker may be used when a product is impossible to mark (e.g. fruits, vegetables, etc.).

Arabic language requirement

Importers usually require that manuals for the operation and maintenance of a product be supplied in Arabic.

Electrical standards

Major household appliances (also known as White Goods) must operate on Kuwait's power transmission grid (240 VAC, 50 Hz) without requiring an external transformer. However, this requirement has been deferred for small household appliances (also known as Brown Goods).

Other barriers

The destruction of Kuwait's infrastructure during the war presents additional challenges. For instance, basic systems such as electric power, water, and sewage facilities are still being repaired. Further, pollution levels are high because of debris and oil well fires; and travel to Kuwait is limited.

■ TAXATION

While Kuwait imposes no personal income tax, the profits arising out of any foreign enterprise, operating directly or indirectly through representation, is subject to taxes.

Kuwaiti tax rates range up to 55 percent. Allowable deductions may vary significantly from U.S. practices.

The Commerce Department strongly urges U.S. firms and individuals contemplating commercial activity in Kuwait to seek competent advice on taxation before bidding on projects or entering into joint venture arrangements.

■ TREATIES AND BILATERAL AGREEMENTS

The Overseas Private Investment Corporation (OPIC) and the Kuwait Government have a bilateral agreement for political risk insurance for U.S. firms bidding on major projects.

While no other agreement currently exists, the Kuwait Government has requested consultations with the U.S. Government to negotiate a double taxation treaty.

■ FOREIGN EXCHANGE CONTROL

There are no exchange controls or currency regulations in Kuwait. Banks quote daily rates for U.S. dollar and sterling.

Import licenses, required for most imports, are granted freely with the exception of a few products such as arms, ammunitions, and alcohol. Capital, interest, royalties, earnings, and net profits may be freely remitted abroad.

Notes

6 ANALYSIS OF MAJOR MARKET SECTORS

The business climate in Kuwait is encouraging for U.S. firms. Postwar restoration activities coupled with Kuwait's wealth (due to oil reserves) have created an attractive market for most businesses.

The Kuwait Government has planned large development and investment projects to revive Kuwait. Some of these projects include:

- Renovation and modernization of oil facilities.
- Expansion of petroleum industries.
- Construction of new buildings, bridges, facilities (medical, etc.), housing, and transportation systems.
- Improvement of communication systems.

In addition to creating primary demand in the respective industries, these projects will create a demand for products and services in other ancillary industries such as heavy machinery, building and construction equipment, and so on.

This chapter analyzes five major market sectors that present maximum potential to businesses and individuals. The market sectors analyzed in the chapter include:

- Oil and petrochemical
- Chemicals and catalysts
- Medical equipment and pharmaceuticals
- Telecommunications
- Textiles and apparel.

■ OIL AND PETROCHEMICAL SECTOR

Kuwait's 90 billion barrel oil reserve is among the largest in the world after Saudi Arabia. A major government objective is to add value to this crude oil by producing refined products and petroleum-based petrochemicals, and to minimize the export of crude oil.

In addition to exporting crude oil, Kuwait exports approximately 70 percent of its oil production in the form of refined products.

Also, Kuwait operates a low-pressure gas plant that produces almost 2 million metric tons of propane and butane annually.

Kuwait maintains its own tanker fleet, retail sales and distribution network. Further, approximately 5,000 gasoline stations in Western Europe are operated by Kuwait.

The state-owned Kuwait Petroleum Corporation (KPC) and its subsidiaries control and carry out all petroleum exploration, production, refining, and marketing. The KPC is the primary end user for the oil and gas field equipment and services consumed in Kuwait.

Demand

Since the production and distribution of oil and gas are major sources of national income, Kuwait is expected to continue spending substantially on the development and modernization of its oil and gas sector.

Reconstruction of oil wells will create a demand for products and services related to oil and gas exploration, drilling, production, and laying pipeline.

Market access

The Central Tenders Committee controls the contract and projects awards for the oil companies. Specific opportunities are published as tender announcements in the *Official Gazette*. These opportunities are usually open to all local and foreign firms registered with the Vendor's Evaluation Committee at the Kuwait National Petroleum Company (KNPC).

Firms wanting to participate in this segment will need a local agent or partner. Further, such firms must register with the Central Tenders Committee (write to the Secretary General at the address in Appendix E under "Kuwait Contacts") as suppliers to the oil and petrochemical sector.

The Central Tenders Committee forwards all applications to the Vendor's Evaluation Committee at the KNPC. Pre-qualified firms remain registered with KNPC indefinitely.

Promotion opportunities

Trade show participation is usually an effective way to promote a firm's products and services, especially in international countries. Two important trade shows for the oil and petrochemical industry are:

- The Oil and Gas Regular Catalog Exhibition held annually in Kuwait.
- The Middle East Oil Show held biannually in Bahrain.

For up-to-date information about trade promotion opportunities in Kuwait, contact the Commerce Department, International Trade Administration, Regional Export Development Center (see Appendix E under "U.S. Contacts").

U.S. position

U.S. equipment dominates the oil and gas exploration, drilling, production, and pipeline equipment markets—the

U.S. market share in these areas amounts to 54 percent of Kuwait's total imports in this sector. Further, the Kuwaitis actively seek and utilize U.S. pumps and other oil and gas equipment. The Japanese are regular suppliers of pipes, tubes, and fittings.

■ CHEMICALS AND CATALYSTS SECTOR

The Kuwait National Petroleum Company (KNPC) and the Kuwait Oil Company (KOC) are the end users for most chemicals and catalysts used in Kuwait.

Demand

Kuwait's oil industries consume large amounts of chemicals and catalysts—worth approximately $120 million annually. This rate of consumption can be expected to increase as oil production resumes and the expansion planned for the petrochemical industry moves forward.

Market access

Kuwaiti oil companies can purchase chemicals and catalysts directly from foreign suppliers for purchases below $20,000. The $20,000 limit does not apply to sole source suppliers. For other purchases exceeding $20,000, the oil companies are required by law to seek bids through publicly announced tenders.

The oil and petroleum companies invite potential suppliers to pre-qualify for opportunities that may arise in the future. (For registration information, refer to the "Oil and petrochemical sector" discussion earlier under "Market access".) Specific opportunities are published as tender announcements in the *Official Gazette*. These opportunities are usually open to all local and foreign firms registered with the Vendor's Evaluation Committee at the KNPC.

U.S. position

In the past, a limited number of U.S. firms have attempted to pre-qualify for a position on the official tenders list.

Firms with capabilities in this sector are encouraged to register with the KNPC in order to pursue Kuwaiti opportunities in this industry segment.

■ MEDICAL EQUIPMENT AND PHARMACEUTICALS SECTOR

All Kuwaitis receive free Medical care and services through the Ministry of Public Health medical facilities located throughout the country. There are five regional hospitals, nine specialized centers, and six small private hospitals.

There are also 62 dispensaries and polyclinics, 57 dental clinics, 22 mother-care and 25 child-care centers. The total number of hospital beds in 1987 was 6,220. In pre-war terms, this number was expected to rise to 7,350 by year 1990.

The Ministry of Public Health controls the country's medical services. Therefore, it is the primary end user for most medical equipment, hospital supplies, and pharmaceutical products.

Demand

Kuwait's total spending for health care is expected to grow to $1.2 billion by year 2000. This number represents approximately five percent of the national budget.

The Ministry of Public Health spends over $70 million annually on imported medicines and drugs. This number does not include imports by private pharmacies and hospitals.

An on-going demand exists for several products including:

- Gauze, bandages, cotton and other disposables.
- Electrical and radiological equipment.
- Medical instruments.
- Hearing aids.
- Orthopedic equipment, artificial body parts, etc.

Market access

Kuwait's medical equipment and pharmaceutical markets can be accessed primarily through the Ministry of Public

Health since it controls the country's medical services. Because it purchases medical products from local agents, these agents play an important role in influencing the ministry's purchase decisions.

U.S. position

Available statistics indicate that Kuwait's total import of medical and hospital supplies and equipment in 1984 was $93.8 million—the U.S. share being $18.2 million or 19 percent.

Fierce competition exists in this segment among U.S., British, French, West German, Italian, and Japanese firms. U.S. firms have a sizable (though not the largest) market share for electrical apparatus and radiology equipment, and for orthopedic equipment. The British are major suppliers of other medical and pharmaceutical products, and the West Germans are strong in dental and surgical equipment and hospital beds.

■ TELECOMMUNICATIONS SECTOR

Telecommunications services in Kuwait include telephone, cable, telex, facsimile, video text, and data bank. These services, which are under the control of the Ministry of Communications and Transport, are constantly being upgraded and expanded.

A main telecommunications center and six regional centers serve the country. A communications tower, currently under construction, will become the third tallest telecommunications tower in the world when it is completed.

Kuwait's telecommunication industry currently consists of:

- 24 telephone exchanges with a capacity of 461,600 lines.
- Three earth satellite stations with a capacity of 1,160 telephone and six TV channels.
- A maritime earth station affording ship-to-shore telecommunications on five telephone, 22 telex, and two safety circuits.

Demand

The Commerce Department estimates that Kuwait's telecommunications industry purchases approximately $25 million in goods and services annually. There are potential opportunities in the following areas:

- Electronic exchanges, microwave links, fiber optics, and components and equipment supporting these systems.
- Installation of telephone exchanges, pulse-code modulation, digital microwave systems, optical fiber links (as part of an integrated digital communications system linking 16 telephone exchanges),

- Installation of a telecommunications network monitoring service, a computerized central control system for telephone network, a fiber optic submarine cable between Kuwait and Bahrain.
- Improvements to underground cables.
- Installation and maintenance of telephone cables in areas not covered by an improvement program.
- Repair of the Kuwait-Saudi Arabia coaxial cable.
- Modernization of the telecommunications network for the Ministry of the Interior.

■ TEXTILES AND APPAREL SECTOR

In spite of its small population, Kuwait presents an attractive market for U.S. textiles and apparel manufacturers and distributors.

With almost no indigenous clothing manufacturing industry, Kuwait imports most of its consumption—approximately $500 million in 1986. This segment is a fairly open market with minimal tariff barriers (Kuwait imposes a nominal import duty on most apparel items).

Demand

Kuwaitis are very fashion conscious despite the fact that most people wear traditional Arab-style clothes.

Kuwaitis demand the latest styles for travel abroad, social events, and sporting activities. A demand also exists for up-market and designer towels, bedding, draperies, and curtains.

Apparel products with promising sales prospects include: fabrics woven from nylon and other synthetic fibers; textile yarn and thread; woven cotton fabrics; silk fabrics; woven woolen fabrics; towels; bed linens and table cloths; curtains; outer garments; men's and boys' shirts; socks and stockings; etc.

Market access

The best way to access this market is through trade promotion opportunities including:

- The annual fashion and apparel trade show held in Kuwait.
- The exposition for women's and men's wear, fabrics, home textiles, toys, and fashion accessories held each year in Dubai.

Notes

7 GENERAL INFORMATION ABOUT KUWAIT

This chapter provides general information about Kuwait's geography, people, government, economy, communications, defense forces, work week, entry requirements, and the cultural do's and dont's.

■ GEOGRAPHY

Total land area: 17,820 km^2 (6,880 mi^2), which is slightly smaller than the state of New Jersey.

Boundaries: Land: 462 km (287 mi) total; 240 km (149 mi) with Iraq and 222 km (138 mi) with Saudi Arabia.

Sea: 499 km (310 mi) of coastline.

Principal cities: Hawalli, Kuwait City (capital), Salimiyah.

Territorial disputes: Iraq disputes ownership of Warbah and Bubiyan islands; Saudi Arabia disputes ownership of Qaruh and Umm al Maradim islands.

Climate: Dry desert; intensely hot summers; short, cool winters.

Terrain: Flat to slightly undulating desert plain.

Natural resources: Petroleum, fish, shrimp, and natural gas.

Land use: 8% meadows and pastures; 92% desert plain.

Environment: Kuwait's desalination facilities are some of the world's largest and most sophisticated.

■ PEOPLE

Population: 2,123,711 (1990), including 27.9% Kuwaiti nationals.

Ethnic division: 27.9% Kuwaiti; 39% other Arab; 9% South Asian, 4% Iranian, 20.1% other.

Religion: 96% Muslim; 4% Other (including Christian, Hindu, and Parsi).

Language: Official language is Arabic; English is widely spoken.

Labor force (1986): 566,000 (70% are non-Kuwaiti), which breaks down as follows: 45% services, 20% construction, 12% trade, 8.6% manufacturing, 2.6% finance and real estate, 1.9% agriculture, 1.7% power and water, 1.4% mining and quarrying, 6.8% other.

Organized labor: Labor unions exist in the oil industry and among government workers.

Discretionary income: The Kuwaiti society is one of product consumers. Having one of the world's highest per-capita income levels, the country's citizens enjoy a large measure of discretionary income. It is not uncommon for each Kuwaiti household to possess multiple televisions and radios, other electronic products, as well as own three or more automobiles.

■ GOVERNMENT

Official name: State of Kuwait.

Capital: Kuwait City.

Type of government: Nominal constitutional monarchy.

Administrative divisions: Four governorates; Al Ahmadi, Al Jahrah, Al Kuwayt, Hawalli.

Independence: June 19, 1961 from the UK.

Constitution: November 16, 1962 (some provisions have been suspended since August 29, 1962).

National holiday: National Day, February 25.

Executive branch: Amir, prime minister, deputy prime minister, Council of Ministers (cabinet).

Legislative branch: National Assembly; dissolved July 3, 1986.

Judicial branch: High Court of Appeal.

Leaders: Amir Sheikh Jaber al-Ahmad al-Jaber Al-Sabah
Prime Minister and Crown Prince Sheikh Saad al Abdullah al-Salem Al-Sabah

Diplomatic representation: Ambassador Sheikh Saud Nasir Al-Sabah Chancery at:
2940 Tilden Street, N.W.
Washington, DC 20008
(202)966-0702.

Ambassador Edward W. Gnehm Jr
Embassy at:
Bneid al-Gar 13001 Safat
P.O. Box 77, Safat, Kuwait
(965)242-4151 through -4159.

■ ECONOMY

Overview: The oil sector dominates the economy. Of the countries in the Middle East, Kuwait has oil reserves second only to those of Saudi Arabia. Earnings from petroleum products generate over 90 percent of both export and government revenues and contribute about 40 percent to the Gross Domestic Produce (GDP).

Most of the non-oil sectors are dependent upon oil-derived government revenues to provide infrastructure development and to promote limited industrial diversification.

The pre-war economy was heavily dependent upon foreign labor—Kuwaitis made up less than 20 percent of the labor force. The early years of the Iran-Iraq war pushed Kuwait's GDP well below its 1980 peak; however, during the period 1986-88, GDP increased each year, rising by five percent in 1988.

Gross domestic product: $20.5 billion, per capita $10,500; real growth rate 5% (1988).

Exports: $7.1 billion (F.O.B., 1988); commodities (90% oil).

Imports: $5.2 billion (F.O.B., 1988); commodities (food, construction material, vehicles and parts, clothing).

Industries: Petroleum, petrochemicals, desalination, food processing, salt, construction.

Agriculture: Virtually none; dependent upon imports for food. About 75% of potable water must be distilled or imported.

Currency: Kuwaiti dinar (KD); 1 KD = 1,000 fils.

Electric power supply: 240 VAC 50 Hz.

Weights and measures: Metric system.

■ COMMUNICATIONS

Highways:	3,000 km (1,864 mi) total; 2,500 km (1,554 mi) bituminous; 500 km (311 mi) earth, sand, light gravel.
Pipelines:	Crude oil, 877 km (545 mi); refined products, 40 km (25 mi); natural gas, 165 km (103 mi).
Ports:	Ash Shuwaikh, Ash Shuaiba, Mina al Ahmadi
Merchant marine:	51 ships; includes 18 cargo ships, 5 container ships, 5 livestock carriers, 18 oil tankers, and 5 liquefied gas ships.
Civil air:	19 major transport aircraft.
Airports:	Eight total; four usable; four with permanent-surface runways; none with runways over 3,659 m (12,000 ft); four with runways 2,440 to 3,659 m (8,000 to 12,000 ft); none with runways under 2,439 m (8,000 ft).
Telecommunications:	Excellent international telecommunications (pre-war); adequate domestic facilities; 258,000 telephones; three AM and two FM radio stations; three TV stations; three satellite and one maritime earth station (one Indian Ocean INTELSAT, two Atlantic Ocean INTELSAT, one INMARSAT, and one ARABSAT); coaxial cable and radio relay to Saudi Arabia.

■ DEFENSE FORCES

Branches: Army, Navy, Air Force, National Police Force, National Guard.

Defense expenditures: 5.8% of GDP, or $1.2 billion (FY89).

■ TIMES AND DATES

Local time: Greenwich Mean Time (GMT) plus three hours.

Hours of business Saturday through Thursday (six day week); weekly holidays are Thursday afternoon and Friday (Islamic weekend).

■ ENTRY REGULATIONS

Visas are required for all foreigners, except the nationals of Bahrain, Qatar, Saudi Arabia, The United Arab Emirate, and British passport holders whose place of birth or country of residence is in the UK or Channel Islands.

Business visas are issued to business-sponsored applicants either from the Department of the Ministry of the Interior in Kuwait, a Kuwaiti consulate, or an authorized Mission abroad.

Visa applications should be made at least 15 days prior to the desired travel date.

A visitor's visa usually requires a resident-sponsor, which can be a local agent or a prospective agent. Those without such contacts can request sponsorship by one of the major hotels operating in Kuwait, for example, the Sheraton, Kuwait International, Holiday Inn, or Ramada Inn.

Transit visitors who are able to provide an onward air ticket may usually stay in Kuwait for not more than 72 hours without a visa or visitor permit. Such authorization may be obtained at all entry/exit points.

Prior to travelling to Kuwait, it is recommended that you contact the U.S. Department of Commerce (see Appendix E under "U.S. Contacts"), to remain informed of any restrictive travel advisories.

■ CULTURAL DO'S AND DONT'S

■ When doing business across international boundaries and cultures, it is suggested that you understand the foreign country's cultural norms and expectations.

The basic Kuwaiti cultural do's and dont's guiding your behavior in public and while conducting business are summarized below.

DO'S

- ☐ Send your top representative.
- ☐ Give your representative the authority to make on-the-spot decisions.
- ☐ During negotiations, maintain strong eye contact with your Kuwaiti counterpart.
- ☐ Arabs are masters of flattery—do not hesitate to compliment them.
- ☐ Attempts to use the Arabic language are always appreciated.
- ☐ Be sure to have an interpreter available during all business meetings.
- ☐ Always dress professionally and avoid casual attire, such as shorts, especially during business situations.
- ☐ Kuwaiti women wear traditional Arab dress and expect a degree of chauvinism.
- ☐ Be patient—the Arab culture has a different concept of time.
- ☐ "Yes" is usually indicated by twisting the head from side to side. "No" is usually expressed by tilting the head back and making a clicking sound with the tongue.
- ☐ Express criticism tactfully to save face and to leave maneuvering room.

- ☐ Be respectful, but not in humble or servile manner.
- ☐ Avoid alcohol.

DONT'S

- ☐ Never eat with your left hand. In Arab cultures, the left hand is considered the toilette hand.
- ☐ Do not abruptly turn away from your Kuwaiti hosts.
- ☐ Refrain from active participation in political discussions; be a passive listener if necessary.
- ☐ Do not point the soles of your feet at others when you cross your legs.
- ☐ Polite conversation about your wife or family is never appropriate.
- ☐ Do not accept a simple "yes" or "no" as a promise. If repeated or emphasized sufficiently, then you can accept it at face value.
- ☐ The Kuwaitis are generally fluent in English, but keep your sentences short and avoid slang to be certain that you are being understood.
- ☐ Avoid western-style informality in the personal and business context.

Appendix A: What Was Damaged and Needs Restoration

The types of infrastructure facilities, complexes, and systems damaged in Kuwait during the war and requiring restoration efforts include the following:

- Airports and runways
- Bridges, highways, and roads
- Chemical processing plants
- Cold storage facilities
- Communications and computers
- Correctional facilities
- Dams, waterways, and irrigation systems
- Desalination plants
- Equipment
- Harbors and piers
- Hospitals, housing, and furnishings
- Industrial and public utilities
- Petroleum facilities
- Public buildings and schools

- Railroad facilities
- Religious buildings
- Security and fire protection facilities
- Waste treatment facilities
- Waterway structures.

Notes

Appendix B: Major Industry Segments

The following industry segments are expected to provide maximum potential for business, employment, and investment opportunities to rebuild Kuwait:

- Computers—to replace the business systems either destroyed or ransacked by the Iraqis.

- Construction—to repair physical damage and to rebuild high-rise buildings, government offices, factories, bridges, and highways destroyed during the war.

- Petrochemical—to rebuild oil installations and to restore crude oil production.

- Telecommunications—to rebuild the country's military, commercial, and private communications capacity.

- Transportation—to rebuild the transportation networks and to re-supply the vehicles and support equipment for those systems.

- Aerospace—to replace the government's airplanes and support equipment.

- Others—to satisfy the demand for commodity and other products (See Appendix C for a list of products and services that are expected to be in demand while rebuilding Kuwait).

Notes

Appendix C: Kuwait Opportunities—Products and Service Classes

The following products and services are expected to be in demand during the reconstruction of Kuwait.

- Aerial photogrammetry
- Airports, navigation aids, airport lighting, aircraft fueling
- Airport terminals, hangers, freight handling
- Barracks, dormitories
- Bridges
- Chemical processing, storage
- Cold storage, refrigeration, fast freeze
- Communications systems, television, microwave
- Computer facilities, computer service
- Construction management
- Cost estimating
- Dams, dikes, levees
- Desalination process, facilities
- Educational facilities, classrooms

- Fire protection
- Garage, vehicle maintenance facilities, parking decks
- Gas systems, propane, natural
- Geologic studies, foundations
- Harbors, ship terminal facilities
- Highways, paved surfaces
- Hospital, medical facilities
- Housing facilities
- Industrial buildings, manufacturing plants
- Industrial waste treatment
- Irrigation, drainage
- Landscape architecture
- Lighting systems
- Office buildings, industrial parks
- Ordnance, munitions, special weapons
- Petroleum, fuel storage, distribution
- Pipelines, liquid, gas, cross-country
- Planning, site, installation, project
- Power generation, transmission, distribution
- Prisons, correctional facilities

- Railroad, rapid transit
- Rehabilitation buildings, structures, facilities
- River, canal, waterway systems, flood control
- Security systems, intruder, smoke detection
- Seismic designs, studies
- Sewage collection, treatment, disposal
- Surveying, plotting, mapping, flood plain studies
- Storm water handling, facilities
- Telephone systems, rural, mobile, intercom
- Traffic, transportation engineering
- Utilities, gas, steam
- Warehouses, depots
- Water supply, treatment, distribution systems.

Notes

Appendix D: Subcontractors to the U.S. Army Corps of Engineers

During Phase I of the reconstruction plan, the Kuwait Government awarded the U.S. Army Corps of Engineers a $46 million contract (since increased to $100 million) to perform the initial war damage assessment and to oversee the reconstruction engineering work in Kuwait.

The initial contracts made by the Corps on behalf of the Kuwaiti reconstruction project have been awarded to:

- Al Harbi Trading and Contracting Co., Ltd., Riyadh, Saudi Arabia—repair roads and airport runways.
- American Dredging Co., Camden, NJ—expedient survey of Shu'Aibh Port.
- Blount International, Montgomery, AL—emergency electrical repairs; temporary repairs to public buildings.
- Brown and Root International, Houston, TX—temporary repairs to public buildings.
- Khudair Group, Al Khabar, Saudi Arabia—repairs to key government offices.
- Mohamed A. Kharafi, Abu Dhabi, UAE—temporary repairs to public buildings.
- Raytheon Service Company, Burlington, MA—acquisition of airport equipment.
- Shand Construction Ltd, Derbyshire, England—repairs to sanitary and water systems.

Other subcontractors to the U.S. Army Corps of Engineers include:

American International, U.S.A.

Dillinghauz, U.S.A.

Fishback & Moore, U.S.A.

Harbart, U.S.A.

GEC Marconi, U.K.

Weir Westgarth, U.K.

Costain, U.K.

Biwater, U.K.

Wimpey, U.K.

Al-Harbi, Saudi Arabia

Al-Hugayet, Saudi Arabia

Al-Suwadi, Saudi Arabia

Ballast - Nedam, Dutch

J & P, Cypr U.S.A.

Turner Company, U.S.A.

Perini, U.S.A.

Morrison & Knudson, U.S.A.

Lilley, U.K.

Edmund Nutall, U.K.

Laing, U.K.

Higgs & Hill, U.K.

Sogea, France

Bebi, Brothers, U.K.

Zachry, Saudi Arabia

Gulf Deep, United Arab Emirate

Zamil, Saudi Arabia

Bouyguas, France

Notes

Appendix E: Directory of Key Contacts

Note: The individuals, addresses, telephone and telex numbers identified below as contact points within Kuwait were valid before the Iraqi invasion of Kuwait and are provided here for information only.

In the event you are unable to reach a contact, you can obtain updated contact information through:

For Kuwaiti Contacts
Kuwait Emergency and Recovery Program ....(202)508-0250/0251

For U.S. Contacts
Gulf Reconstruction Center ....(202)377-5767/5737

KUWAITI CONTACTS

Central Bank of Kuwait
Abdullah al-Salem Street,P.O. Box 526, Safat 449200/449219
Telex 22101/22173/22118 KT
Cable KUMARBANK

Central Tenders Committee
P.O. Box 1070, Safat, Kuwait 13011 .... (965)240-1200
Telex 44048 CTC KT
Secretary General: Mr Nayef Al-Maosharji

Chamber of Commerce and Industry
P.O. Box 775, Chamber's Building, Ali Salem Street 433864

Chancery
2940 Tilden Street N.W., Washington, DC 20008 .... (202)966-0702
Ambassador: Sheikh Saud Nasir Al-Sabah

Kuwait Emergency and Recovery Program
1510 H. Street N.W., Washington, DC 20005 ....(202)508-0250/0251
Fax (202)508-0280
Dr Abdulhadi al-Awadi
Dr Ibrahim Majid al-Shaheen

KUWAITI CONTACTS (Continued)

Kuwait Petroleum International
80 New Bond Street, London, England 44-71-491-4000
Fax 44-71-493-7996
Mr Hani-Hussein
Khalid al-Fulail
Abdultourif al-Toureh

Touristic Enterprises Company KSC
P.O. Box 23310, Safat 412060
Telex 22801 Trent CO

MINISTRIES

AWQAF and Islamic Affairs
Khalid Bin Walid Street, P.O. Box 13, Safat 425710
Minister: Ahmad Saad Al Jasser

Commerce and Industry
Fahad al-Salem Street, P.O. Box 2944 ....422101/411201
Telex 22682
Minister: Jassem Al Marzouk

Communications and Transport
Jamul Abdul Nasser Street 819033/439091
Telex 22313/22197
Minister: Isa Al Mazidi

Defense
Jahara Road, P.O. Box 1170, Safat 439331
Fax (965)561-8397, Telex 22784 ENGDEPT KT
Minister: Sheikh Salem Al-Salem Al-Sabah

Education
Commercial Area 9, Hilali Street, P.O. Box 7 427041
Minister: Yacoub Yousef Al Ghunaim

Electricity and Water
Mubarak al-Kabeer Street, P.O. Box 12 & 54 433821
Telex 22051 Electric KT
Minister: Khalaf Ahmad Al-Khalaf

Finance
Fahad al-Salem Street, P.O. Box 9, Safat 439001
Telex 22527

KUWAITI CONTACTS (Continued)

Foregin Affairs and Information
Al-Sour Street, P.O. Box 3, Safat 422401
Telex 22042 Kharijia KT
Minister: Deputy Premier, Sheikh Sabah Al-Ahmad Al-Jaber Al-Sabah

Housing, Labor and Social Affairs
Arabian Gulf Street, Slamiyah, P.O. Box 2935, Safat 617033
Minister: Hamad Isa Al Rujaib

Interior
First Ring Road, Shamiyah, P.O. Box 4, Safat 816111
Telex 22507 Interpol KT
Minister: Sheikh Nawaf Al-Ahmad Al-Jabir Al-Sabah

Ministry of Justice
Abdullah al-Mubarak Street, P.O. Box 6, Safat 435044
Minister: Sheikh Salman Al Duaij Al-Sabah

Oil
Fahad al-Salem Street, P.O. Box 5077, Safat 415201
Minister: Rasheed Al-Amiri

Planning
P.O. Box 15, Safat, Kuwait 13001 .... (unknown)
Fax (965) 2430477, Telex 22468 KT
Minister: Sulaiman Al-Mutawa
Director, Consultants Department: Mrs Wafa'a Al-Majed

Public Health
Commercial Area 3, P.O. Box 5, Safat 431911
Telex 22729
Minister: Abdul Rahman Abdullah Al-Awadi

Public Works
Mubarak Al Kabeer Street, P.O. Box 8, Safat 43515
Fax (965) 2424335, Telex 22753 Ashghal KT
Minister: Abdullah Al Rushaid
Chief Engineer, Roads Administration: Ali Al-Abdullah
Deputy Chief Engineer, Major Projects Department: Bader Al-Qabendi

U.S. CONTACTS

GOVERNMENT ORGANIZATIONS

COMMERCE DEPARTMENT

Gulf Reconstruction Center
Room H-2039, 14th Street & Constitution Ave N.W., Washington, DC 20230
Counselling and Referral Services .... (202)377-5767/5737
Office of the Near East .... (202)377-2515/5767
Fax (202)377-5330
Director: Karl Reiner
Kuwait Desk Officer: Corey Wright
USFCS Kuwait: Paul Scogna

International Trade Administration
International Economic Policy Unit
Room 2039, HCHB
Washington, DC 20230 .... (202)377-2515/5767
Fax (202)377-5330
Desk Officer - Kuwait: Corey Wright
U.S. and Foreign Commercial Service .... (202)377-5777
.... or (800)343-4300
Commercial Specialist, U.S. Embassy: Kamal Zaher
Commercial Attache, U.S. Embassy: B. Paul Scogna
Commercial Officer, Riyadh: Dirck Teller .... (966)488-3800
Fax (966)488-3237
Commercial Officer, Dhahran: Carmine D'Aloisio .... (966)891-3200
Fax (966)891-8332
Aerospace Industry Products & Services .... (202)377-8231
Auto Affairs & Consumer Goods .... (202)377-2422
Chemicals & Allied Products .... (202)377-0128
Computers & Business Equipment .... (202)377-2053
Construction Equipment, etc. .... (202)377-5023
Export Administration & General Information .... (202)377-0706
Forest Products & Domestic Construction .... (202)377-0384
International Construction .... (202)377-2373
Metal, Minerals, & Commodities .... (202)377-0575
Microelectronics & Instrumentation .... (202)377-2587
Service Industries .... (202)377-5261/1421/1443
Telecommunications .... (202)377-4466
Textiles & Apparel .... (202)377-5153
Kuwait Desk Officer .... (202)377-2515
Office of Antiboycott Compliance .... (202)377-2381
Office of the DAS for Basic Industries, Room H-4043 .... (unknown)
Office of Major Projects .... *(202)377-5225*
Regional Export Development Center, Room H-1510 ... (202)377-1209/5179
Alan Sterling
John Flannagan

U.S. CONTACTS (Continued)

DEFENSE DEPARTMENT

U.S. Army Corps of Engineers
Middle East Division, Middle East/Africa Projects Office, Attn: CESAI-ED-MC
P.O. Box 2250, Winchester, VA 22601 . . . .(703)665-3692/3667/3674
Architecture and Engineering (Gary Kula) . . . . (703)665-3798
Construction (Cecil Hutchinson) . . . . (703)665-3632
Supply Firms . . . . (703)665-3683
Public Affairs Office . . . . (703)665-3936

LABOR DEPARTMENT
Employment Hot Line . . . . (800)927-5690

STATE DEPARTMENT

American Embassy Kuwait
Bneid al-Gar 13001 Safat, P.O. Box 77, Safat . . . . (965)242-4193
Fax (965)240-7368
Ambassador: Edward W. Gnehm, Jr.
Commercial Attache: B. Paul Scogna . . . .(965)242-4192
Commercial Specialist: Kamal Zaher
Bureau of Consular Affairs Travel Advisory . . . . (202)647-5225
Economic & Business Information . . . . (202)647-1942
Travel Advisory . . . . (202)647-0900

TRESUARY DEPARTMENT
Office of the General Counsel . . . . (202)566-5569

OTHER ORGANIZATIONS

Overseas Private Investment Corporation
1615 M Street N.W., Washington, DC 20527 . . . . (202)457-7200
Fax (202)331-4234
Investment Develpment Center . . . . (202)223-3514
Investment Development Associate: John Hereford

Saudi Aramco
P.O. Box 4530, Houston, TX 77210-4530 . . . . (800)827-5700
ASC Employment Department

U.S.-Arab Chamber of Commerce
1625 I Street N.W., Washington, DC 20206 . . . . (202)331-8010
President: J.R. Abinader

Notes

Appendix F: USFCS Offices

The following offices are part of the United States Foreign Commercial Services (USFCS) in Washington D.C., and can provide trade specific information for each industry listed below. Contact the appropriate USFCS office in order to obtain trade specific information, or to obtain help in exporting your products or services

USFCS HEADQUARTERS **(202)377-5777 or (800)343-4300**

Industry Specific USFCS Offices

Aerospace Industry Products & Services .... (202)377-8231
Auto Affairs & Consumer Goods .... (202)377-2422
Chemicals & Allied Products .... (202)377-0128
Computers & Business Equipment .... (202)377-2053
Construction Equipment, etc. .... (202)377-5023
Export Administration & General Information .... (202)377-0706
Forest Products & Domestic Construction .... (202)377-0384
International Construction .... (202)377-2373
Kuwait Desk Officer .... (202)377-2515
Metal, Minerals, & Commodities .... (202)377-0575
Microelectronics & Instrumentation .... (202)377-2587
Service Industries ....(202)377-5261/1421/1443
Telecommunications .... (202)377-4466
Textiles & Apparel .... (202)377-5153

The USFCS contacts for obtaining assistance in exporting your products or services include:

Kuwait Desk Officer .... (202)377-2515
Export Administration & General Information .... (202)377-0706
Regional Export Development Center, Room H-1510,
HCHB, Alan Steeling ....(202)377-1209/5179

U.S. Department of Commerce, International Trade Administration, U.S. and Foreign Commercial Service District Offices

ALABAMA
2015 2nd Ave North
Birmingham 35203
(205)731-1331

ALASKA
222 West 7th Ave
Anchorage 99513
(907)251-5041

ARIZONA
230 North 1st Ave
Phoenix 85025
(602)379-3285

ARKANSAS
320 W. Capital Ave
Little Rock 72201
(501)378-5794

CALIFORNIA
11000 Wilshire Blvd
Los Angeles 90024
(213)209-7104

116A W. 4th St
Santa Ana 92701
(714)836-2461

6363 Greenwich Dr
San Diego 92122
(619)557-5395

450 Golden Gate Ave
San Francisco 94102
(415)556-5860

COLORADO
1625 Broadway
Denver 80202
(303)844-3246

CONNECTICUT
450 Main St
Hartford 06103
(203)240-3530

DELAWARE
Serviced by Philadelphia

DISTRICT OF COLUMBIA
14th St & Constitution Ave, N.W.
Washington, DC 20230
(202)377-3181

FLORIDA
51 S.W. First Ave
Miami 33130
(305)536-5267

128 North Osceola Ave
Clearwater 34615
(813)461-0011

FLORIDA - Continued
3100 University Blvd South
Jacksonville 32216
(904)791-2796

University of Central Florida
Orlando 32802
(407)648-1608

197 W. Gaines St
Tallahassee 32304
(904)488-6469

GEORGIA
4360 Chamblee Dunwoody Rd
Atlanta 30341
(404)452-9101

120 Barnard St
Savannah 31401
(912)944-4204

HAWAII
300 Ala Moana Blvd
Honolulu 96850
(808)541-1782

IDAHO
700 W. State St
Boise 83720
(208)334-3857

ILLINOIS
55 East Monroe St
Chicago 60603
(312)353-4450

W.R. Harper College
Palatine 60067
(312)397-3000x2532

515 North Court St
Rockford 61110
(815)987-8123

INDIANA
One North Capitol Ave
Indianapolis 46204
(317)226-6214

IOWA
210 Walnut St
Des Moines 50309
(515)284-4222

KANSAS
727 North Waco
Wichita 67203
(316)269-6160

KENTUCKY
601 W. Broadway
Louisville 40202
(502)582-5066

LOUISIANA
No. 2 Canal St
New Orleans 70130
(504)589-6546

MAINE
77 Sewall St
Augusta 04330
(207)622-8249

MARYLAND
40 South Gay & Lombard Sts
Baltimore 21202
(301)962-3560

MASSACHUSETTS
World Trade Center, Suite 307
Boston 02210
(617)565-8563

MICHIGAN
477 Michigan Ave
Detroit 48226
(313)226-3650

300 Monroe N.W.
Grand Rapids 49503
(616)456-2411

MINNESOTA
110 S. 4th St
Minneapolis 55401
(612)348-1638

MISSISSIPPI
300 Woodrow Wilson Blvd
Jackson 39213
(601)965-4388

MISSOURI
7911 Forsyth Blvd
St Louis 63105
(314)425-3302

601 East 12th St
Kansas City 64106
(816)426-3141

MONTANA
Serviced by Boise

NEBRASKA
11133 "O" St
Omaha 68137
(402)221-3664

NEVADA
1755 E. Plumb Ln
Reno 89502
(702)785-5203

NEW HAMPSHIRE

Serviced by Boston

NEW JERSEY

3131 Princeton Pike
Trenton 08646
(609)989-2100

NEW MEXICO

625 Silver S.W.
Albuquerque 87102
(214)767-0542

1100 St Francis Dr
Santa Fe 87503
(505)827-0264

NEW YORK

111 West Huron St
Buffalo 14202
(716)846-4194

111 East Ave
Rochester 14604
(716)263-6480

26 Fed. Plaza, Rm 3718
New York City 10278
(212)264-0634

NORTH CAROLINA

324 W. Market St
Greensboro 27402
(919)333-5345

NORTH DAKOTA

Serviced by Omaha

OHIO

550 Main St
Cincinnati 45202
(513)684-2944

668 Euclid Ave
Cleveland 44114
(216)522-4750

OKLAHOMA

6601 Broadway Extension
Oklahoma City 73116
(405)231-5302

440 S. Houston St
Tulsa 74127
(918)581-7650

OREGON

121 S.W. Salmon St
Portland 97204
(503)326-3001

PENNSYLVANIA

475 Allendale Rd
King of Prussia 19406
(215)962-4980

1000 Liberty Ave
Pittsburgh 15222
(412)644-2850

PUERTO RICO

Fed. Bldg, Rm G-55
San Juan 00918
(809)766-5555

RHODE ISLAND

7 Jackson Walkway
Providence 02903
(401)528-5104

SOUTH CAROLINA

1835 Assembly St
Columbia 29201
(803)765-5345

9 Liberty St
Charleston 29424
(803)724-4361

SOUTH DAKOTA

Serviced by Omaha

TENNESSEE

404 James Robertson Pkwy
Nashville 37219
(615)736-5161

301 E. Church Ave
Knoxville 37915
(615)549-9268

22 North Front St
Memphis 38103
(901)544-4137

TEXAS

1100 Commerce St
Dallas 75242
(214)767-0542

816 Congress Ave
Austin 78711
(512)482-5939

515 Rusk St
Houston 77002
(713)229-2578

UTAH

324 South State St
Salt Lake City 84111
(801)524-5116

VERMONT

Service by Boston

VIRGINIA

400 North 8th St
Richmond 23240
(804)771-2246

WASHINGTON

3131 Elliott Ave
Seattle 98121
(206)442-5616

West 808 Spokane Falls Blvd
Spokane 99201
(509)353-2922

WEST VIRGINIA

405 Capitol St
Charleston 25301
(304)347-5123

WISCONSIN

517 E. Wisconsin Ave
Milwaukee 53202
(4140291-3473

WYOMING

Serviced by Denver

Notes

Appendix G: Selected U.S. Firms Doing Business in Kuwait

Here is a list identifying selected American businesses with offices in Kuwait or those who are participating in some form of joint venture or franchise relationship with Kuwait firms.

This list is current as of October 1989 and was compiled by the U.S. Foreign and Commercial Service (USFCS) office at the U.S. Embassy in Kuwait.

ALGHANIM - BARWILL SHIPPING COMPANY

P.O.BOX 21708 Safat, 13078 Kuwait
Capt Peter Wakley - General Manager
Tele: 4842988/4943988
Fax: 48445712
Telex: 22084 BARWIL KT

U.S. Office: SEA LAND SERVICES, INC.
10 Parsonage Road
Edison, New Jersey 08830
Tele: 201-632-2000
Telex: 844432

ACTIVITY: Shipping, chartering, freight forwarding.

AMERICAN BUREAU OF SHIPPING

P.O. BOX 4896 Safat, 13049 Kuwait
Sergio Coletta - Surveyor for Kuwait
Tele: 2551805/2553939
Fax: 2553939
Telex: 23180 RECORD KT

U.S. Office: AMERICAN BUREAU OF SHIPPING
45 Eisenhour Drive
P.O. Box 910
Paramus, NJ 07653-0910
Tele: 201-368-9100

ACTIVITY: Third party inspection.

AMERICAN EXPRESS INTERNATIONAL

Al-Ghanim Travel
PO Box 27238, Safat, 13133 Kuwait
Abdul Kader Inkidar - General Manager
Tele: 2413000/2413323/2437646
Fax: 241332
Telex: 30941 AEXP KT

U.S. Office: AMERICAN EXPRESS
Travel-Related Services Inc
American Express Tower
World Financial Center
New York, NY 10285

ACTIVITY: Charge cards, traveller's checks.

AMERICAN LIFE INSURANCE

P.O. Box 669 Safat, 13007 Kuwait
PO Box 27238, Safat, 13133 Kuwait
Abdul Rashid Manaa
Tele: 2435113/2442542/2443217
Telex: 22472 ALICO KT

U.S. Office: AMERICAN LIFE INSURANCE CO, INC.
P.O. Box 2226
Wilmington, Delaware 19899

ACTIVITY: Insurance - life, group, accident.

THE ARCHITECTS COLLABORATIVE

P.O. Box 23548 Safat, 13096 Kuwait
Raad Almumayiz - Regional Manager
Tele: 2410841/2411874
Telex: 22926 TAC ME KT
FAX: 2410821

U.S. Office: THE ARCHITECTS COLLABORATIVE, INC.
46 Brattle Street
Cambridge, MA 02138

ACTIVITY: Consultants, planner, interior designers, and landscape.

ARTHUR YOUNG & COMPANY

P.O. Box 2115 Safat, 13022 Kuwait
Ghazzi Shehabi - Manager, Partner
Tele: 2410010/17 & 2452684
Telex: 22264 BBCO KT
FAX: 2412761

U.S. Office: ARTHUR YOUNG INTERNATIONAL, INC.
277 Park Avenue
New York, NY 10172

ACTIVITY: Accountants and auditors.

AVIS RENT-A-CAR

P O Box 24519 Safat, 13106 Kuwait
E.A. Cunningham - General Manager
Tele: 2453828/9
Telex: 46195 AVIS KT

U.S. Office: AVIS RENT-A-CAR SYSTEMS, INC.
900 Oil Country Road
Garden City, NY 11530

ACTIVITY: Car rental, leasing, chauffer services.

BASKIN-ROBBINS

Kuwait Food Company or AMERICANA
P O Box 5087 Safat, 13051 Kuwait
Mu'taz Adel AL-Alfi - General Manager
Tele: 4815900/4815323
Telex: 22123 Nutrition Kuwait

U.S. Office: BASKIN-ROBBINS ICE-CREAM CO
31 Baskin Robbins Road
Glendale, CA 91201

ACTIVITY: Ice cream and frozen desserts.

BAUSCH & LAMB

HASSAN SADAT YAZDI OPTIC. COMPANY
P O Box 1139 Safat, 13012 Kuwait
Hassan Sadat Yazdi - General Manager, Owner
Tele: 2414238/2439631/2421818 (D)
Telex: 23417 AHBAB KT
Fax: 2321815

U.S. Office: BAUSCH & LAMB, INC.
1400 N. Goodman Street
Rochester, NY 14692

ACTIVITY: Optician, contact lens, optical equipment.

BOEING COMPANY

P.O. Box 20510 Safat, 13066 Kuwait
Larry Cromoga - Representative
Tele: 4716350/434777/666 Extn. 1375
Telex: 31951 KAC KT

U.S. Office: BOEING COMMERCIAL AIRCRAFT COMPANY
P O Box 3707
Seattle, WA 98124

ACTIVITY: Aircraft engineering services.

CAMBRIDGE ARCHITECTS INTERNATIONAL, INC.

Fahad Engineering Consulting Services
P O Box 700 Safat, 13007 Kuwait
Alan E. Calegary - Director, CEO
Tele: 2408593/94
Telex: 44387 FUTOUH KT
Fax: 00965-575-9036

U.S. Office: CAMBRIDGE ARCHITECTS INTERNATIONAL, INC.
1033 Massachusetts Avenue
Cambridge, MA 02138

ACTIVITY: Architectural, engineering, consultants, planners, landscape, interior designers, security systems.

CANADA DRY-KUWAIT COMPANY

P O Box 3022 Safat, 13031 Kuwait
Fouad Al-Khateeb - General Manager
Tele: 4834411/4834745
Telex: 46240 KT

U.S. Office: CANADA DRY CORP.
Old Truck Road
Greenwich, Conn. 06832

ACTIVITY: Soft drinks and juices.

CARRIER INTERNATIONAL CORP.

P O Box 15168 Dahiya, Kuwait
Inge Bjurenlind - Regional Manager
Tele: 2450487/4810860
Telex: 46825 CARME KT

U.S. Office: CARRIER INTERNATIONAL CORP.
P O Box 4806
Syracuse, NY 13221

ACTIVITY: Airconditioning.

CHAS T MAIN INTERNATIONAL, INC.

P O 260085 Safat, 13120 Kuwait
Edmond Ghantous - General Manager
Tele: 3950127/3950224
Telex: 30005 ZOURLES KT

U.S. Office: THE CHAS T MAIN INTERNATIONAL, INC.
Prudential Center
Boston, MA 92199

ACTIVITY: Engineering services, construction management.

CONTINENTAL AIRLINES

Al-Kazemi Travel Agencies
P O Box 23959 Safat, 13100 Kuwait
Mahmud Shatat - General Manager
Tele: 2450655/11
Telex: 44523 KT

U.S. Office: CONTINENTAL AIRLINES
2929 Allen Parkway
Houston, TX 77019

ACTIVITY: Travel and related services.

CROWN PACIFIC LTD.

P O Box 22045 Safat, 13081 Kuwait
Dennis D'Souza - General Manager
Tele: 2424860/2424859
Telex: 46163 CPKWI KT
Fax: 2428575

DAMES & MOORE

P O Box 26346 Safat, 13124 Kuwait
Ray Jones - Senior Engineer
Tele: 2432769
Telex: 44479 DAMEMOR KT

U.S. Office: DAMES & MOORE
445 South Sigueroa Street Suite 3500
Los Angeles, CA 90071

ACTIVITY: Environmental and applied earth-sciences consultants.

DE LEUW CATHER INTERNATIONAL LTD.

P O Box 25582 Safat, 13116 Kuwait
Albert Stoner - V.P.
Tele: 5331460
Telex: 30475 DELACAC KT

U.S. Office: DE LEUW CATHER INTERNATIONAL LTD.
1211 Connecticut Avenue, N.W.
Washington, D.C. 20036

ACTIVITY: Engineering consultants, construction management.

DHL INTERNATIONAL TRANSPORTATION

P O Box 26523 Safat, 13126 Kuwait
Steve Bushby - General Manager
Tele: 2442375/2461723
Telex: 44881 DHLA KT

U.S. Office: DHL AIRWAYS, INC.
1000 Cherry Avenue, Suite 55
San Bruno, CA 94066

ACTIVITY: Courier services.

DRESSER (KUWAIT) SAK

P O Box 4544 Safat, 13046 Kuwait
John Davis - Managing Director
Tele: 3262455/6/7
Telex: 44911 DRESSER KT
Fax: 3262434

U.S. Office: DRESSER INDUSTRIES, INC.
601 Jefferson Street
P O Box 6507
Houston, TX 77005

ACTIVITY: Drilling muds and chemicals.

ENGINEERING-SCIENCE, INC.

P O Box 1006 Shuiba, 65451 Kuwait
Mark Guthrie - Project Manager
Tele: 3260102

U.S. Office: ENGINEERING-SCIENCE, INC.
75 North Fair Oaks,
Pasadena, CA 91109

ACTIVITY: Environmental engineering services.

ERNEST & WHINNEY

P O Box 74 Safat, 13008 Kuwait
Philip Duke - Project Manager
Tele: 2452880
Fax: 2456419
Telex: 23125 ERNST

U.S. Office: ERNEST & WHINNEY
2000T - National City Center
Cleveland, OH 44114

ACTIVITY: Financial and taxation consultant.

GETTY OIL COMPANY

P O Box 1 Mina Zour, 65051 Kuwait
Lloyd Austin - President
Tele: 3950003/3950444
Fax: 3950126
Telex: 23074 GETTY KT

U.S. Office: TEXACO, INC.
2000 Westchester Ave., Harrison
White Plains, NY, NY 10650

ACTIVITY: Oil production.

HALLIBURTON COMPANY

P O Box 9022 Ahmadi, 61001 Kuwait
Vladimir Bohachevsky - District Manager
Tele: 3981178
Fax: 3989172
Telex: 44214 HALL KT

U.S. Office: HALLIBURTON SERVICES, INC.
1051 Bois Darc Street
Duncan, Oklahoma 73536

ACTIVITY: Oil well services company

INGERSOLL-RAND

P O Box 5461 Safat, 13055 Kuwait
Usama Salami - District Manager
Tele: 5312090
Fax: 5333889
Telex: 23636 ALTAFCO KT

U.S. Office: INGERSOLL-RAND
200 Chestnutridge Road
Woodcliff lake, NJ 07675

ACTIVITY: Pumps, compressors, turbines, motors, insulation.

HONEYWELL KUWAIT

P O Box 20825 Safat, 13069 Kuwait
George Koudim - Manager
Tele: 2421327/9
Fax: 2428315
Telex: 22218 HONEYWELL KT

U.S. Office: HONEYWELL, INC.
200 Honeywell Plaza
Minneapolis, MN 55408

ACTIVITY: Industrial process controls.

IBM

P O Box 4175 Safat, 13042 Kuwait
Joseph Degeorgi - General Manager
Tele: 5653000
Fax: 5658352
Telex: 22245 IBM KT R

U.S. Office: IBM WORLD TRADE CORP.
200 Hamilton Ave.,
White Plains, NY 10601

ACTIVITY: Data Processing equipment, data services.

J A JONES CONSTRUCTION COMPANY

P O Box 700 Safat, 13007 Kuwait
Alan Calgeri - Director
Tele: 2408593
Fax: 2408593
Telex: 44387 FUTOUH KT

U.S. Office: J A JONES CONSTRUCTION COMPANY
World Trade Headquarters
One South Executive Park
6060 St Albans street
Charlotte, NC 28287

ACTIVITY: Construction, project management, industrial process control, energy, heavy marine and transportation.

KAY & ASSOCIATES, INC.

P O Box 36479 Al-Rass, 24755 Kuwait
Donals Snooks - Maintenance coordinator
Tele: 5952950

U.S. Office: KAY & ASSOCIATES, INC.
1638 S Arlington Heights road
Barstow, CA 92311

ACTIVITY: Aviation, engineering & support.

KUWAIT SANTA FE BRAUN TRANWORLD CORP.

P O Box 25161 Safat, 13112 Kuwait
Miles Sheldon - VP
Tele: 5652950
Fax: 4714983
Telex: 23050 SFBRAUN KT

U.S. Office: SANTA FE BRAUN TRANWORLD CORP.
1000 S Freemont Ave.,
Alhambra, CA 91802

ACTIVITY: Oil and gas exploration and development.

KUWAIT TRANSCONTINENTAL SHIPPING COMPANY

P O Box 25431 Safat, 13115 Kuwait
Bo Peterson - General Manager
Tele: 2423752
Fax: 2403823
Telex: 23275 KT

U.S. Office: AMERICAN PRESIDENT LINES, INC.
1800 Harrison Steet,
Oakland, CA 94612

ACTIVITY: Shipping.

LOCKHEED AIRCRAFT SERVICES CORP.

P O Box 302 Safat, 13004 Kuwait
D.E. Miller - General Manager
Tele: 4711588
Telex: 23082 SHYHAWK KT

U.S. Office: LOCKHEED AIRCRAFT SERVICES CORP.
P.O.Box 33 Steet,
Ontario, CA 91761

ACTIVITY: Maintenance, support, training for lockheed aircraft used by the air force.

MAG INTERNATIONAL, INC.

P O Box 27190 Safat, 13132 Kuwait
Alan Calgary - Director
Tele: 2408593
Fax: 2408459
Telex: 30987 BSI KT

U.S. Office: MAG INTERNATIONAL, INC.
P.O.Box 1121
Manassas, VA 22110

ACTIVITY: Security systems, design, development, implementation, detection and alarm systems, maritime security and dock security. crisis management, etc..

MCDONNELL DOUGLAS

P O Box 24204 Safat, 13103 Kuwait
Paul Wilcott - Manager
Tele: 4711588
Telex: SKYHOCK 23082 KT

U.S. Office: MCDONNELL
3855 Lakewood Blvd.
Long Beach, CA 90846

ACTIVITY: Aviation services and support of the Kuwait air force.

MERRILL LYNCH, PIERCE, FENNER, & SMITH, INTERNATIONAL LTD.

P O Box 4906 Safat, 13050 Kuwait
Giries Qassis - General Manager
Tele: 2420102
Fax: 2458647
Telex: 22149 MERLEAP KT

U.S. Office: MERRILL LYNCH, PIERCE, FENNER, & SMITH, INTERNATIONAL LTD.
1 Liberty Plaza, 165 Broadway
NY, NY 10080

ACTIVITY: Securities exchange, portfolio management.

MID-GULF INDUSTRIAL CONSULTANTS

P O Box 24312 Safat, 13104 Kuwait
Mohmud Dajani - Managing Director
Tele: 5315946
Telex: 25589 MIDGULF KT

U.S. Office: MID-GULF INDUSTRIAL CONSULTANTS
Wilmington, DE 19081

NATIONAL CASH REGISTER

P O Box 2952 Safat, 13030 Kuait
Aadib Swaires - General Manager
Tele: 2413070
Fax: 2420930
Telex: 22059 NCR KT

U.S. Office: NCR CORP.
Dayton, OH 45479

OMI CORP.

P O Box 9059 Safat, 61001 Kuwait
Richard Harville - Regional Director
Tele: 3927124

U.S. Office: OMI CORP.
P O Box 5169 Kingwodd, CA
Tele: 713-358-9135
FAX: 713-358-5840

ACTIVITY: Operations and management of Riqqa Sewage Treatment Plant.

OTIS ELEVATOR COMPANY

ARABIAN GULF BRANCH
P O Box 11169 Dasmah, 35152 Kuwait
Mohamed M. Rasheed - Managing Director
Tele: 2445506
Telex: 22557 OTIS KT
Fax: 2464862

U.S. Office: UNITED TECHNOLOGIES
OTIS ELEVATOR INTERNATIONAL
4 place de La Defense, Cedex 26
92090 Paris La Defense
Tele: (1) 47 96 63 36

ACTIVITY: Elevators.

PAN AMERICAN AIRWAYS

P O Box 76 Safat, 13010 Kuwait
Mrs. Naela Hakim - Sales Manager
Tele: 2420401/2412851
Telex: KWITO PA

U.S. Office: PAN AMERICAN WORLD AIRWAYS, INC.
200 Park Avenue
New York, NY 10166

ACTIVITY: Air passenger service.

PEPSI-COLA

Kuwait National Bottling Company
P O Box 224 Safat, 13003 Kuwait
Adnan Al-Dabagh - General Manager
Tele: 4717157
Fax: 4714392
Telex: 23069 KT

U.S. Office: PEPSI-COLA INTERNATIONAL, INC.
New York, NY 10577

ACTIVITY: Soft drinks, juice, soft drink containers manufacturer.

PRATT & WHITNEY AIRCRAFT GROUP

Kuwait Airways Group
P O Box 528 Safat, 13006 Kuwait
Gerald E. Prentice - Representative
Tele: 4744649
Fax: 4744649

U.S. Office: UNITED TECHNOLOGIES/PRATT & WHITNEY AIRFRAFT GROUP, INC.
400 Main Steet
East Hanford, CT 01609

ACTIVITY: Aircraft engines and maintenance facilities.

RAYTHEON GULF SYSTEMS COMPANY

P O Box 33147 Safat, 73452 Kuwait
William A. Morgan - Program Manager
Tele: 5513180/4710985
Fax: 5513190

U.S. Office: RAYTHEON COMPANY
Missile Systems Division
350 Lowell Steet
Andover, MA 01810

ACTIVITY: Military contractor - air defense.

RAYMOND OFFSHORE CONSTRUCTORS

c/o TECHNIPETROL, INC.
P O Box 36972 Ras Salmlyah
Michael Holmes - Project Control Manager
Tele: 5643568/5643583
Telex: 4620558 77227

U.S. Office: RAYMOND OFFSHORE CONSTRUCTORS, INC.
A Subsidiary Of RAYMOND INTERNATIONAL, INC.
2801 Post Oak Blvd.
P O Box 22718
Houston, TX

ACTIVITY: Construction contractor.

ROCKWELL INTERNATIONAL

c/o SAS Kuwait Hotel
P O Box 26199 Safat, 13122 Kuwait
M.S. Akhtar - Project Manager - Kuwait Programs
Tele: 5657000
Fax: 5652999
Telex: 44306

U.S. Office: ROCKWELL INTERNATIONAL
Collins System International
P O Box 10462
Dallas, TX 75207

ACTIVITY: Tactical communications products and systems.

SAFETY INTERNATIONAL, INC.

P O Box 46849 Fahaheel, 64019 Kuwait
Phil Graves - President
Tele: 3912539
Telex: 46902 SFTCNT KT

U.S. Office: SAFETY INTENATIONA, INC.
6040 HWY. 80W
P O Box 6180
Midland, TX 79701

ACTIVITY: Safety services, consulting engineering and equipment.

AL-SALEH, GRAHAM & JAMES

P O Box 3246 Safat, 13033 Kuwait
Anis F. Qassim or Ms. Reema Ali
Resident Lawyer/Partner
Tele: 2443442/2467670
Fax: 2431039

U.S. Office: GRAHAM & JAMES
Alcoa Building, 3rd. Floor
1 Maritime Plaza
San Francisco, CA 94111

ACTIVITY: Law firm.

SANGAMO GROUP

P O Box 1107 Salmiyah, 22012 Kuwait
Allan Reyhan - CEO
Tele: 4732714/4732480
Telex: 46362 WZSN KT

U.S. Office: SANGAMO GROUP, INC.
P O Box 318
Springfield, CA 62705

ACTIVITY: Construction Contractor.

SEVEN-UP BOTTLING COMPANY OF KUWAIT

P O Box 4076 Safat, 13041 Kuwait
Sami Khashram - General Manager
Tele: 4810057/4810823/4831366
Fax: 4845944
Telex: 23617 SEVENUP KT

U.S. Office: SEVEN-UP BOTTLING COMPANY
100 Park Avenue
New York, NY 10017

ACTIVITY: Soft drinks, juices.

SHERATON CORP. OF AMERICA

Oriental Hotel Company
P O Box 5902 Safat, 13060 Kuwait
Holger Wessel - General Manager
Tele: 2422055
Fax: 2448032
Telex: 22016 SHERATON KT

U.S. Office: SHERATON CORP. OF AMERICA
60 State Steet
Boston, MA 02109

ACTIVITY: Hotels.

STME LTD. (StorageTek)

P O Box 6648 Safat, 22077 Kuwait
Peter Aubrey - Managing Director
Tele: 5627641/5627652/5641911
Fax: 5627652
Telex: 46082 KREPLA C/O STME

U.S. Office: STORAGE TECHNOLOGY CORP.
2270 S 88th.
Louisville, CO 80027
Tele: 303-673-5151

Activity: Plug comptible DASD, tape, printers, solid state disk for IBM or IBM compatible mainframes. Impact printers for DEC and other minis. Tape subsystems for CRAY and UNIVAC.

TOUCHE ROSS INTERNATIONAL

P O Box 1245 Safat, 13013 Kuwait
Usama Tuqan - Manager/Partner
Tele: 2438061/2/3/4
Fax: 2402243

U.S. Office: TOUCHE ROSS, INC.
1633 Broadway
New York, NY 10019

ACTIVITY: Auditors, trade mark.

TURNER - PROJACS

P O Box 25944 Safat, 13120 Kuwait
Gerard Telke - Principal-In-Charge
Tele: 2405749
Fax: 2405742
Telex: 30646 ROJACS

U.S. Office: TURNER INTERNATIONAL
405 Lexington Avenue
New York, NY 10174
Tele: 212-286-8990
FAX: 212-286-0414
Telex: 424619 TCCO UI

ACTIVITY: Construction Managers, Amiri Diwan Site.

TWA (AL-RASHED TRAVEL AGENCIES)

P O Box 241 Safat, 13003 Kuwait
John Shayne - General Manager
Tele: 2410899/2450200
Fax: 2410514
Telex: 44523 GSA KT

U.S. Office: TWA, INC.
Contact: Robert Malak
Title: District Manager
Sales, Kuwait-Arabian Gulf
c/o B.I.T. Bahrain
Tele: 253315

ACTIVITY: Tourism, travel agents, airfreight.

VTN INTERNATIONAL, INC.

P O Box 31076 Sulaibikhat, Kuwait
William Richards - Director of Marketing
Tele: 4874188

U.S. Office: VTN INTERNATIONAL, INC.
2361 Campus Drive, Suite 202
P O Box C 19529
Irvine, CA 92713

ACTIVITY: Engineers, architects planners and construction management.

YORK INTERNATIONAL CORP.

P O Box 244 Safat, 13003 Kuwait
Hamad Abdulla Al Sagar - General Manager
Tele: 481-0655/6
Fax: 4811155
Telex: 22085 ALSAGAR KT

U.S. Office: YORK INTERNATIONAL DIV/BORG-WARNER CORP.
P O Box 1592
York, PA 17405

ACTIVITY: Airconditioning, equipment and service.

Notes

Appendix H: ITA Export Promotion Services

The U.S. Commerce Department's International Trade Administration (ITA) is the primary U.S. Government agency responsible for assisting U.S. firms to export products and services. You can take advantage of these export services by contacting the nearest ITA district office identified in Appendix F. The export services available through the ITA include the following:

- **Agent/Distributor Service**. Customized searches for interested and qualified foreign representatives to identify up to six foreign prospects who have examined the U.S. firm's literature and expressed interest in representing that firm.

- **Commercial News USA**. A monthly news magazine promoting the products or services of U.S. firms to more than 110,000 overseas agents, distributors, government officials, and purchasers. Exporters may submit a black-and-white photo and a brief description of their product or service.

- **Comparison Shopping**. A custom-tailored service providing firms with key marketing and foreign representation information for their specific products or services. The Commerce Department staff conduct on-the-spot interviews to determine key information including sales potential in the market, comparable products, distribution channels, market price, competitive factors, and qualified purchasers.

- **Export Counseling**. Trade specialist are available at the ITA's district and branch offices for individualized export counseling.

- **Foreign Buyer Program**. Exporters can meet qualified foreign purchasers for their product or service at trade shows in the U.S. The Commerce Department promotes the shows worldwide to attract foreign buyer delegations, manages an international business center, counsels participating firms, and brings the buyer and seller together.

- **Gold Key Service**. A custom-tailored service for U.S. firms planning to visit a country. Offered by many overseas posts, it combines several services, such as market orientation briefings, market research, introductions to potential partners, an interpreter for meetings, and assistance in developing a sound market strategy and an effective follow-up plan.

- **Matchmaker Events**. Matchmaker Trade Delegations offer introductions to new markets through short, inexpensive overseas visits with a limited objective: to match the U.S. firm with a representative or prospective joint-venture/licensee partner who shares a common product or service interest. Firms learn key aspects of doing business in the new country and meet with people who can help them be successful there.

- **Overseas Catalog and Video-Catalog Shows**. U.S. firms can gain market exposure for their product or service without the cost of traveling overseas by participating in a catalog or video-catalog show sponsored by the Commerce Department. Provided with the firm's product literature or promotional video, your material is presented to selected foreign audiences in several countries.

- **Overseas Trade Fairs**. U.S. firms may participate in overseas trade fairs which enable them to meet customers face-to-face and also to assess the competition. The Commerce Department creates a U.S. presence at international trade fairs, making it easier for U.S. firms to exhibit and gain international recognition. The Commerce Department selects international trade fairs for special endorsement, called certification. This cooperation with the private show organizers enables U.S. exhibitors to receive special services designed to enhance their market promotion efforts. There is a charge for this service.

- **Overseas Trade Missions**. Officials of U.S. firms can participate in a trade mission which will give them the opportunity to confer with influential foreign business and government representatives. The Commerce Department staff can identify and arrange a full schedule of appointments in each country.

- **Trade Opportunities Program**. Provides U.S. firms with current sales leads from overseas firms seeking to buy or represent their product or service. These leads are available electronically from the Commerce Department and are redistributed by the private sector in printed or electronic form.

- **World Trader's Data Report**. Custom reports that evaluate potential trading partners. Includes background information, standing in the local business community, credit-worthiness, and overall reliability and suitability.

Notes

Appendix I: Firms That Have Won Contracts in Kuwait

Here is a list of small and large firms that have won contracts for business in Kuwait (source: U.S. Commerce Department, April 1991).

3M Co.	AAB Int'l
AAE Systems, Inc.	Aeromaritime, Inc.
Aeromaritime	AI Int'l
Al-Hashar & Co.	American Body Armor
Amida	AMSCO Int'l
Angus Fire	AT & T
Avon Industrial Polymers Ltd	Bard
Beckman	Burke Industries
Caterpillar	Code 3 Public Safety
Colt	Commonwealth Labs
Communications, Inc.	Computer Services Corp
Contractors of America	U.S. Army Corps of Engineers
Cougar Holdings, Inc.	CSX-Sealand
Def-Tec Corp	Erickson GE Mobile Co.
Ethicon	Ford
Gambro	GE Technical Services
GEC Marconi	Global Container Lines
Grove North America	GTS Enterprises

Hydrotechnik	IBM
ICMX	International Exports
International Mobile Machines	International Security
International Hydrocut	IPAC
James Martin Associates	Keel Marine Ltd
La France Equipment Corp	Lynch Display Vans
Mackay Communications	Martin Marietta
Med-Eng Systems, Inc.	Medko
Metltron	Mitel
Mobile Telesystems	Molnlycke
Morfax	Motorola, Inc.
NACO	Navcom
Navistar Int'l	Ohmeda
Prime Tech, Inc.	Proarms
Racal-Tacticom	Ruston
S & W Medico	S.H.A.D.
SePro Healthcare Services	Sherwood Medical
Siemens AG	Simmon Ladder Towers
Societe Des Materiels	Somes' Uniforms Int'l
SORS Int'l	Stryker Corp
Technologies Corp	Technos Int'l
Telemobile, Inc.	The World Bank
The Supply Cabinet	Tradetech
Transac Int'l Ltd	Transportation Corp
Tryco Inc.	United States Testinc Co.
Valdex	Valmet
Water Witch	Zubair Automotive

GLOBAL MARKETING INTELLIGENCE

A Division of Northwest Software, Inc.

FOR ADDITIONAL INFORMATION

To be included on our mailing list for future newsletters, publications, services, or related products, please complete this form. Fold and mail it to the address shown on the reverse side.

Name: ______________________ Title: ____________

Organization: ______________________ Mail Stop: ____________

Street Address: ______________________

City: ____________ State: _____ Zip: ________ Country: ____________

Telephone: (____) ____________ Extension: ______ Fax: (____) ____________

Purchased From: ______________________

Street Address: ______________________

City: ____________ State: _____ Zip: ________

Check the appropriate boxes:

☐ Maintain me on your mailing list for newsletters concerning *Kuwait's Multibillion-Dollar Opportunities* or other related topics.

☐ Send me information on similar guides for other countries as and when they become available. I am most interested in:

- ☐ European Community
- ☐ Japan
- ☐ India
- ☐ Other Pacific Rim Countries: ____________
- ☐ Russia
- ☐ Australia
- ☐ Other Countries: ____________

☐ To help us better serve your needs, your comments about this guide will be appreciated:

____

____

____

Can we quote you? ☐ Yes ☐ No

Your Area of Responsibility

- ☐ Senior Management
- ☐ First or Second Level Manager
- ☐ Individual Contractor
- ☐ Administration
- ☐ Other ____________

Size of Your Organization

- ☐ 1-100
- ☐ 101-500
- ☐ 501-1000
- ☐ Over 1000

Your Organization

- ☐ Construction
- ☐ Manufacturing
- ☐ Financial Services/Banking/Investment
- ☐ Transportation
- ☐ Government
- ☐ Wholesale/Retail Trade
- ☐ Computers
- ☐ Medical/Health Care Services
- ☐ Oil/Petrochemical
- ☐ Training/Education
- ☐ Professional Service/Consultant
- ☐ Other ____________

FOLD DOWN AND TAPE AFTER COMPLETING FORM

FOLD AND TAPE

PLACE
NECESSARY
POSTAGE
HERE

Global Marketing Intelligence
A Division of Northwest Software, Inc.
P.O. Box 91396
Portland, OR 97291-0396